The Tale of a

Cheltenham Lady

The Tale of a Cheltenham Lady

ELIZABETH GILLARD

Matador
5 Weir Road
Kibworth Beauchamp
Leicester LE8 0LQ, UK
Tel: (+44) 116 279 2299
Fax: (+44) 116 279 2277
Email: books@troubador.co.uk
Web: www.troubador.co.uk/matador

ISBN 978 1848761 483

British Library Cataloguing in Publication Data.
A catalogue record for this book is available from the British Library.

Typeset in 11pt Bembo by Troubador Publishing Ltd, Leicester, UK

Matador is an imprint of Troubador Publishing Ltd

For Tom and Edward

Part 1

I should have gone to the local grammar school – that would have been far more straightforward. But it wasn't to be. Fate intervened, in the form of an ancient source of revenue; a summit was called and a decision taken. Whether I liked it or not, I was to be educated at Cheltenham Ladies' College, if it would accept me, in the town of my birth, destined to start a journey intended to transform me from an ordinary Cheltenham girl to a Cheltenham Lady.

The elegant Regency town, steeped in history, became prominent in the nineteenth century as a fashionable place to visit, where the smart elite would take the beneficial spa waters and enjoy the air of gentle exclusivity and class. Among various notable persons who visited, Charles Dickens thought it delightful, as did Lord Tennyson, who lived in the town for some years. Gustav Holst was born in the town, together with Edward Wilson, who died on Scott's ill-fated expedition to the Antarctic, and both are commemorated with statues.

I remember Montpellier, dominated by the spectacular green-domed Rotunda, the site of one of the town's original spas. As you meandered down the smart parade you were scrutinised by graceful figures of shapely women in loose gowns, who presented a touch of elan to the town. You carried on to the Imperial Gardens, resplendent with vividly coloured carpets of flowers, where the members of the brass band blew their trumpets and clashed their cymbals on Sunday afternoons – onward to the Queen's Hotel which reigned supreme at the top of the endless Promenade, and finally to the Victorian architectural masterpiece of the Ladies' College, nestling gently in the centre of the town, quietly confident in its reputation as an institution of educational excellence. Neptune's fountain gushed enthusiastically in front of the Regal cinema, the intoxicating aromas of freshly ground coffee beans from the Cadena café tantalised the nostrils, and tea dances were held every afternoon when elderly aristocrats would take to the floor and dream of the old days of the raj – gin in the morning and cocktails at night – when Britain ruled the world. The palm-court orchestra played, and time, for a while, stood still.

We explored the Pump Room and swam in the freezing cold of the Sandford Lido, boated on the gently lapping lake in Pittville and played tennis in Montpellier, to be followed by a visit to the ice-cream cart, parked coolly and temptingly amongst the majestic lime trees of the boulevard. We eager girls would walk in groups to the Boys' College sports ground to watch county cricket matches, and ogle muscular and beautiful young men and boys in immaculately creased virgin whites. The batsman, waiting to receive a delivery, staunchly guarded his evenly placed bails, poised to run like a streak of mercury as leather thwacked willow, hoping not to be dismissed for a disappointing duck. The bowler, ball tight-in-hand, advanced towards his target, an accelerating run as from tortoise to hare. The wicket-keeper – eyes fixed rigidly on the calculated trajectory of the ball to come. Fielders crouched, silent, alert, ready to pounce. Like cats, stalking their prey. Such memories.

Our home was in Suffolk Square – a gracious and imposing Square of baroque Victorian eighteenth and early nineteenth century terraces and houses, resplendent with their stucco facades. Vividly coloured magnolias and honeysuckles snaked up to intricately carved balconies. An overall air of impeccable breeding and an aura of gentility. This elegant part of Cheltenham had become a desirable area for members of the comfortable upper echelons of society, such as retired army officers, wealthy aristocrats, or, occasionally, less wealthy aristocrats who had fallen on hard times but wished to continue to live in the manner to which they had become accustomed. All very English, very respectable, and very 'proper.'

The Square surrounded the bowling green, home of the Bowling Club. The clubhouse and the green would buzz with activity in the summer, the warm hazy air alive with the gentle sound of wood on wood, the distant approving murmurs floating across in the breeze as a wood rolled across the green towards the jack, with louder roars of congratulation for a direct hit.

A retired air-commodore lived in the adjoining flat. His sister had emigrated to America, and would send 'the little girl next door' magnificent Christmas presents, of a quality totally unfamiliar in a poverty stricken post-war Britain. I can recall my astonishment to find a perfect china doll in a parcel, or a wooden box containing a hundred differently coloured crayons, or a viewfinder – a revolving gadget into which you placed photographic slides, which would miraculously transport you to a world hitherto unknown or dreamed about. You looked with wonder at three dimensional images of people and places in other countries, becoming aware of a world beyond your own insularity, as photographs of the Golden Gate Bridge or the Grand Canyon unfolded in extraordinary detail before your eyes.

The church verger lived in the flat below us, her constant costume a severe black suit and black bowler hat perched precariously on top of her black hair, scraped back mercilessly into a round black bun. Nature had endowed her with a Romanesque nose of epic proportions. She would hover at the rear of St. James like a massive bird of prey, waiting to swoop on her unsuspecting flock to peck out a miscreant sinner.

On the opposite side of the Square from our flat was one of the Ladies' College boarding houses, which regularly expelled numbers of pea-green girls onto the streets and pavements. They were usually immaculately behaved and walked in restrained couples, but occasionally the exuberance of youth would overcome obedience of the rules, and the crocodiles would dissipate as the young scholars shifted gently into untidy groups, some with heads down, minds on their studies, and others lighthearted, giggly, spirited, but all intent on their journey to or from their academy of learning. Hockey or lacrosse sticks swung jauntily from the shoulder, soon to become weapons of combat as their owners commenced their violent and vocal combat against the enemy, bent only on scoring victory and honour in their appointed sports. The required uniform was green serge for winter, green gingham for summer, hats for church attendance – green felt in winter, straw panama for summer.

There was a large home for elderly gentlemen and gentlewomen in one corner of the Square. We did not see the residents too often, they were old and tired, they had lived the best part of their lives. Some of the more agile went to church, vying for position with my mother for a post-service conversation with the vicar. Some, mainly the ladies, elegantly adorned in their best frocks and hats, would attend the annual church fête, maybe to buy an ice-cream or a raffle ticket. They would aspire to meet the vicar again, indulge in conversation with other residents of the Square, perhaps even buy some crab apple jelly for their tea.

Adjoining the Square was Suffolk Parade. In the nineteen-fifties it was an ordinary shopping street with essential shops such as a butcher, baker, fishmonger, grocer, and ironmonger. In the grocer's shop enormous hams and cheeses were laid out on the front counter, and you could always taste a slice or a square before buying, all purchases were placed in cardboard boxes. When you paid for the goods, the money was transported in a tubular object, on wires which went up to the ceiling and circumnavigated the room, before arriving next door where the cashier was waiting, cash box to hand. Your change would then be replaced in the tube and the process would be reversed, as it jumpily traversed back to the grocer and the customer, patiently waiting at the counter. This activity was so very exciting to a small child, and when the day came I was allowed to shop by myself and have my own change from the magic tube, it signified an important rite of passage from child to girlhood.

We lived at 5 Suffolk Square, halfway along one of the terraces, in the middle-floor flat. It consisted of one enormous drawing room, which doubled as the main bedroom, adjoined by another large bedroom, which was mine. The room was dark and dingy, and the only window looked out on to a brick wall, nothing but bricks; bricks to wake up to, bricks at bedtime, bricks to dull the mind and the spirit. I had a huge Victorian four poster bed with large knobs on each corner and was scared of the dark, though I should have been well acclimatised to it.

You went up a long flight of grey dank stairs, embellished with a handsome balustrade to hang onto in the gloom, before reaching a depressing little kitchen on the upper floor. It had one small window, overlooking the same brick wall, but from a greater distance, so you had the added vista of a small section of sky. The facilities were sparse, with one large solid wood work surface, which, when lifted, revealed a large Victorian claw-footed bath beneath. The room was tiny, and cooking, or any similar activity, extremely hazardous. On one occasion my mother roasted a joint of meat and placed the still-boiling cooking fat on the floor, there being nowhere else for it to go. As a small and lively child, I turned round too quickly, lost my footing and fell, landing unceremoniously in the tin of hot malodorous cooking fat, badly scalding a leg from toes to thigh.

The lavatory was immediately next to the kitchen – I can't remember a washbasin anywhere so it was the kitchen sink or nothing. Mice lived under the bath, so we got a cat. He was scared of them!

The entire flat was numbingly cold and depressingly dark. Heating was non-existent except for one two-bar electric fire, over which you shivered and crouched in order to get dressed each morning. Chilblains were common, itchy, and painful. As there was nowhere to do any washing of clothes, they were parcelled up once a week and taken to the Chinese laundry in the High Street. Some articles must have been washed by hand, because I remember manning one side of the mangle, heaving the heavy iron handle round to wring out the surplus water, while my mother barked instructions from the other side, like a verbally explosive sergeant-major tormenting his men into compliance on the parade ground.

The verandah outside the drawing room was lovely in the summer, giving us welcome fresh air, except that it had a large hole in the roof, which for some reason was never repaired during the nineteen years we lived there. From this balcony we had an extensive view of life in the

Square, centering on the bowling green, a huge expanse of green and as smooth as a billiard table, enclosed by a thick privet hedge of verdant richness, keeping cats and children outside, and the club members inside, in their select privacy. You felt as if you were looking down on a stage from the dress circle.

The Square was enormous to a child, the sky as if it had been part of its design, an entity in itself, changing daily from blue, cloudless and still, to lively and vivid, resplendent with a plethora of greys, pinks, and whites, with ever-varying cloud formations which would sail across the vast space, like white sails on a clipper of old.

Life was spartan and barren in more ways than those material. Unfortunately my mother and father did not converse for the entire nineteen years of their marriage, stoically tolerating each other, living as independently as was possible under the same roof, speaking only when necessary. The atmosphere was quiet, tense, devoid of feeling, of animation.

There was little social life and few family friends, few books, no music, and limited conversation between ourselves or other people. Friends from school could not be asked home without embarrassment, because the way we lived seemed so alien to the way others lived. Little encouragement or interest in my achievements was forthcoming from my mother, whether the accomplishments were large or small, because her philosophy always was "one should have done better." In spite of our family peculiarities, every day presented new challenges and life was too full of activity for overlong meditation. My mother must have become increasingly aware of the dearth of educational material or intellectual stimulus at home, because as soon as she realised that she was likely to become the mother of a Ladies' College pupil, she foresaw her responsibilities, as she aspired to reach the exacting standards required of a mother with a daughter at College.

She ordered an excellent publication called *The Children's Newspaper* for me, which provided information and articles of interest on all subjects. It also ran competitions, and if you were fortunate you might win a book or a Parker fountain pen. The standard of newspaper reading, compared with the previous reading of comics, was a definite step up the literary ladder, progressing from *Eagle*, with the gripping adventures of *Dan Dare*, meant for the boys, or the more feminine counterpart called, extremely unimaginatively, *Girl*. Facts were becoming interspersed with fiction, and I was rapidly beginning to learn about a wider world.

Books became the elixir of life, taking you to a world of new horizons and images and thoughts, far away from the smallness and insularity of your existence. A trip to the library became a weekly expedition, and I remember the long walk down to the High Street to borrow as many books as allowed. Fortunately they were often given as birthday and Christmas presents, as were book tokens, giving you the thrill of making your own choice. When the delightful and carefree days of *Winnie the Pooh, Alice, Mrs Tiggy-Winkle* and *Ratty* and *Mole* drew to a close, most children turned to books such as the adventures of *The Famous Five*. Even if these stories were not, according to the more intellectually-minded literati, written to standards of literary exactitude and perfect phraseology and syntax, the stories were exciting to a child, being tales of secret castles and mysterious islands, and provided the necessary fuel to fire our imaginations and transport us to other worlds.

We navigated the waters of the Lake District with the *Swallows and Amazons* in our dinghy, flag flying, sails aloft and a challenge in every move of the tiller. We cried at the wicked mistreatment of *Black Beauty*. We followed the aspirations of the Fossil sisters at stage school when Great Uncle Matthew abandoned them to follow their separate dreams, and we lived the adventures of *Robinson Crusoe*, shipwrecked on his tropical island. Torches burned up many a battery under the bedclothes, as we departed from the real world, not to sleep, but to float into fantasy and rejoin the stories, which had been temporarily put on one side.

Radio was also a great source of information as well as entertainment. *Children's Hour* every afternoon, exciting serials about journeys into space and childrens' adventures at school. The world came into our living rooms, including news, drama, stories, and music. Crazy comedy shows would convulse us with uncontrollable laughter, whether we were *Going Round The Horne* or *Taking it From Here*. The ridiculous humour portrayed was a perfect antidote to the seriousness of mood in the aftermath of war.

My mother would take me to the Daffodil cinema, fondly named simply *The Daffodil* by local residents. We would sit in the two-and-sixes on the rather grubby seats with a packet of nuts and lose ourselves in fantasy, drama, and romance – generally the showings were of black-and-white British films, made in Pinewood or Ealing – productions of delight and wit and extraordinary characters – *The Lavender Hill Mob, Kind Hearts and Coronets,* Alec Guinness playing not one but every character with infinite skill and credibility. Alistair Sim as the ridiculously-caricatured Head of *St. Trinian's School* for equally ridiculous young ladies, and the indomitable *grande dame* who was Margaret Rutherford, whose manner and forcefulness became, subconsciously, deeply embedded in my mother's psyche. She loved all things Thespian.

Later on, my friends and I would be allowed down to the Regal cinema in the town, a welcome advent into freedom for us, refreshingly unleashed from the bonds of maternal supervision. The films on show there mostly seemed to be about the war – battles galore, submarines, bouncing bombs, and escaping from prison camps – all replete with English officers looking devastatingly handsome in their uniforms, speaking with the immaculate clipped articulation of the Queen's English, and who generally always seemed to be either Richard Attenborough or John Mills, for whom I suffered an adolescent passion of unrequited love.

To lighten the mood, Rodgers and Hammerstein gave us musical films that were loud and colourful and larger than life, and would remain in our imaginations for ever. In Atlanta, the tale of Rhett Butler and Scarlett O'Hara and their attraction to each other was dynamic, and their passion raged as did the fires of Tara. Fred Astaire and Ginger Rogers delighted the senses as they faced the music and danced, and brought us romance and escapism from the dullest day. *Pathe News* kept us informed of events good and bad in the world, and *Tom and Jerry* made children of us all.

★ ★ ★

The decision to send me to the Ladies' College filled me with considerable foreboding and doubt. Was there really any way I could benefit from such an exclusive and privileged education? The College was renowned for its academic excellence. I felt very ordinary, and neither of my parents could boast any remarkable academic achievement. We moved in humble circles – not possessing a car, or any of the usual material trappings of middle to upper-class society. We were as poor as the proverbial church mice in monetary terms, and also bereft of the honorary position in society generally afforded by good breeding and aristocratic background.

How could I hold my head high alongside the offspring of the landed gentry from the Shires, so well-endowed with their country estates and their vast acreages, their hunting, shooting, fishing, black labradors, and Barbour jackets?

Many of the aristocratic young ladies of Gloucestershire in the nineteen-fifties would, at the completion of their education, be catapulted into high society as debutantes, attending dances and social evenings in the hope of finding a husband of suitable pedigree and status. These glittering events were much heralded affairs which formed an integral part of the partying life of the elite. Mothers seeking acceptable sons-in-law would ruthlessly propel their daughters towards families who were in possession of a potential candidate, the greater the number of acres owned the more desirable, and a double-barrelled surname could clinch the deal.

In truth, perhaps this particular young lady would meet her future husband in this manner? Her mother would have been delighted at such an outcome, but this Cinderella did not have a suggestion of the required background, and never would, however forcibly the transparencies of social finesse were instilled. Despite passing the required eleven-plus examination, I was of only average ability academically, and certainly had not achieved admission to the College through any bursary or scholarship.

Of course it is a truth universally acknowledged that in matters of education it is the duty of parents to decide which school is likely to be most suitable for their child. Hence, with no discussion between these particular parents and child, the die was cast, a fait accompli, and they decided to apply for a place at the Ladies' College – a school whose ethos of excellence in education and equal opportunity for women was largely evolved by Miss Dorothea Beale, who became headmistress in its earliest days and remained there for most of her working life, establishing the College as one of the finest seats of learning in the country for young ladies.

Miss Beale had met another teacher, Miss Frances Buss, at Queen's College in London. Both ladies were ardent advocates and pioneers of the suffragette movement, and both wholeheartedly believed in the importance of education for women, and in the equal right for them to go to university. Miss Beale was the founder of a teacher-training college in Cheltenham, and also of Hilda's College in Oxford. Because of their single-mindedness in choosing careers over having families, the two ladies were light-heartedly immortalised in satire, thus –

> Miss Buss and Miss Beale,
> Cupid's darts do not feel,
> Miss Beale and Miss Buss,
> How different from us.

★ ★ ★

My mother had great expectations that her daughter should, as smoothly and painlessly as possible, be transformed into a lady. A good academic attainment was expected, indeed demanded, which would probably extend to a university education. Politics, the law, medicine, at the very least. A good education was the passport to a useful and fulfilling life. Of course she was right.

In preparation for this foray into exclusivity, the social graces were being instilled into me at every opportunity at home. God forbid that I should slip up in any matters of social etiquette, speech, or behaviour. The seeds of ladyship were surely and rigorously being sown.

Herein would lie problems from the very first day of attendance. I was to be a 'day girl', a state of existence treated with mild contempt by the boarding fraternity, newly released from the freedom of their inherited acres. In the supercilious and arrogant manner of over-privileged youth, some of the boarders considered themselves to be superior to we home-grown Cheltonians, who plodded our weary ways home each evening to our bourgeois little houses.

We arrive at this dichotomy. Instead of feeling privileged, unfortunately you felt different, and at a distinct disadvantage. The acquisition of an education intended to give greater opportunity was in fact creating an appreciation of the phenomenon of the haves and the have-nots, and a sense of the great social divide at which you were bottommost.

My parents, of course, thought they were doing the right thing, but in later years I would have loved to have been able to tell them that the local excellent grammar school might have been a better and happier option for their daughter.

How was this possible? How could my parents be in a position to fund such an expensive education over the following five or six years?

★ ★ ★

Part 2

*T*he day of judgement duly arrived, and on one cool autumnal September morning Heather Elizabeth Joan was deposited in her brand new pea-green uniform at the Ladies' College, green with fear, green with uncertainty. Her childish pigtails had been relegated to the floor of Maison Phelps in Cheltenham, to be replaced with a strange-looking coiffure called a razorcut. The disturbance of the hair matched the disturbance in equilibrium.

The level of teaching afforded at the Ladies' College was, without doubt, of the highest. Academic achievement was deemed to be of importance, but not to the detriment of a good general education, and the understanding and appreciation of the world about you.

The foundation and broad scope of knowledge gained was comprehensive. The fundamental elements of algebra and physics were perhaps difficult to comprehend, but the glories of our language, incorporating books, plays, and poetry, by authors both ancient and modern, English or foreign, instigated a lifelong love of literature.

Occasionally, relieving the tedium of serious academic study, the Princess Hall would be transformed into a cinema for the afternoon, an unimaginable treat. Our studies of literature were illuminated and brought to vivid life with the screening of classic films. We empathised with Pip in his terror as Magwitch loomed out of the misty Essex marshes, or gazed in horror as the three witches of Cawdor stirred the evil brew of tongues and toes in their bubbling cauldron. Our hearts were torn in two by Cathy and Heathcliffe on the Yorkshire moors. We pondered on why Mr. Rochester was so secretive and unapproachable. We suffered the travails of Mrs Bennett in her quest to find the perfect husband for her daughters, and we lusted unashamedly after Mr. Darcy. We fought with Richard the Third as the rebellions against him led to the Battle of Boswell Field, and we progressed with Christian's pilgrimage through the despair of his Slough of Despond.

We travelled the world with the National Geographical Society. Natural history films taught us about the habitats and behaviour of every form of wild life. We learned the mating habits of them all. The limits of knowledge seemed endless. The world was an open book.

Religious education, or Scripture as it was known then, was a compulsory subject leading eventually to confirmation classes. The teachings and parables of the Bible were read, marked, learnt, and inwardly digested, thenceforth to be picked up and put down at will throughout life. Music appreciation was taught. We would sit high up in the eaves of the College's extensive buildings, perchance to absorb the subtleties of a concerto or a sonata, but usually with minds diverted to matters less ethereal. A Brahms melody, being played in a music lesson, might drift out over the quadrangle.

Our minds and bodies were duly fortified each day by a welcome midmorning break, sustenance consisting of a currant bun and a third of a pint of milk, drunk from a bottle with a straw. Migraines reared their ugly heads, disturbing my vision and my application to learning. Nobody explained to me what was happening. I thought I was going blind.

My mother had no time for illness. It was all in the mind, she said. I cannot remember her ever complaining of feeling ill. She did not show emotion, rarely laughing, never crying. She was British, you got on with it. Sadly, there always seemed to be impatience and criticism, in no small measure, towards other people's frailties.

Every morning we would line up in front of a prefect to be inspected for cleanliness and neatness of appearance, before proceeding in twos along the long black and white marbled corridor to the Princess Hall for morning assembly. If you had been absent from school due to illness, you were required to report back to the headmistress. This involved walking up on to the podium in front of the staff and eight hundred staring girls, an unnerving experience. We were required to stand rigid and motionless for long periods throughout the prayers, hymns, and notices. Most days a girl or two would gently keel over and descend to the floor, gracefully, as befits a lady, with a gentle thud, creating a welcome and amusing diversion from the solemnity of the proceedings.

High standards in behaviour and in work were expected at all times, and therefore generally prevailed. Disciplinary measures included the writing of 'lines', consisting of 'I must not' – followed by the nature of the transgression, written, with increasingly-aching hand, one hundred times – how tedious this punitive measure was, and such a waste of ink.

The College celebrated its Centenary. Queen Elizabeth the Queen Mother was due to visit in honour of this special occasion. After being thoroughly inspected to ensure that our shoes shone, and that not a hair was out of place, we excitedly approached our delegated areas, lining the path down which she would walk, Brownie cameras at the ready, hoping to catch a good view. She was charming, talked with many of us, and was very interested in what we did, and in the beauty of the gardens.

When King George the Sixth died we said prayers for the monarchy and for Princess Elizabeth, and wore black arm bands for the required period of national mourning. A few months later the historic coronation of Queen Elizabeth took place.

We did not possess a television set at home – very few people did at that time. But my mother knew someone who possessed one of these revolutionary machines. We were invited to join twenty or more people, crammed like sardines into a small living room, extremely excited at the prospect of viewing this marvellous miracle of technology. It seemed barely credible that we could be witnessing an event which was actually happening as we watched. The television set was very small, the picture was blurred and in black and white, but it was still a memorable occasion, with a definitive sense of history being made.

Games were compulsory for Cheltenham Ladies – hockey, lacrosse, cricket, as well as gymnastics, and if the weather was inclement a brisk run round the playing field became the order of the day. Hockey was a game I enjoyed, relieving pent-up inhibitions with the resounding whack of the stick, and such was my aggression that I became a fairly useful left-inner, playing on occasions for the College. This did not particularly impress my mother, as it spoke of achievement of a physical rather than an academically-stretching nature, but my father would occasionally brave the elements to support me on the side line.

All the girls walked for miles, from home to College and back, to the Sports field at Lansdown and back, to places of educational interest in the town and back, and the day girls to the Bayshill Road for lunch, and back. Our pangs of hunger would be duly assuaged by assorted sausages or stews, and stodgy puddings sumptuously steaming with sickly syrup or juicy with jam. Despite this daily excessive intake of carbohydrate, no girl was ever likely to become overweight because of the rigorous and regular exercise which was her due. Nevertheless, the College took its responsibilities to heart, and in order to maintain each Cheltenham lady in tip-top condition, slim of waist, toned and trim, they would regularly weigh and measure you, the resulting figures being meticulously recorded by one of the nubile and lithe gym mistresses. They all wore pleated shorts and had whistles round their necks, and were very hearty and jolly.

Most of us owned bicycles, but the addition of books, satchels, and hockey sticks on board would have made for a dangerously balanced load cycling up and down the Promenade. There were an assortment of social niceties and attributes considered to be desirable in the transition from girlhood to ladyhood, equally as important as academic achievement. To be confident and elegant on horseback was essential. One would probably, when moving in the right social and equine circles, eventually own one's own horse or horses, so one must cut the right figure when mounted, in both style and skill of horsemanship. One could then also grace the local meet with suitable élan, immaculately clad and eager to taste the mandatory one stirrup-cup, or maybe more, before galloping off to follow the master of the hunt and head for the kill.

Riding lessons were therefore forced upon me, and the allocated steed was evil-eyed, steely black, and aptly called *Rocket*. As jet-propelled as his name suggested, he possessed every semblance of a meteor careering through space, without any sense of direction and at uncontrollable speed, his main intention being to throw me to the ground as frequently and untidily as he could. He showed not one ounce of remorse. This short-lived association with the world of the horse resulted in a lifelong fear of anything equine, even to present it with a lump of sugar.

A lady-in-training should also, if possible, possess a musical skill, whether it be a voice trained to sing to the correct pitch and note, or a proficiency at piano or violin. One must also be well-attuned to discuss the various works of particular composers, in order to sensibly converse at musical soirées in high society, and to become an educated concert-goer who knows her sonatas from her symphonies. This attribute, combined with the ability to name and describe a Gainsborough or a Vemeer in a well-informed and thoughtful manner, and to discuss with animation the works of Trollope and Tolstoy, should enable one to converse with aplomb and gravitas in the presence of assorted cognoscenti.

Never one to fail in her responsibilities for my cultural education, my mother therefore arranged private piano lessons, which entailed a long bicycle ride from Suffolk Square to Pittville every Saturday morning. The intensity of trying to coordinate reluctant fingers correctly with the correct notes, and the relentless flash of the black and white keys served only to regularly precipitate a migraine, and I would stagger home on my bicycle, vision wildly zigzagged, to duly vomit. Another endeavour bit the dust, but was resurrected with pleasure later in life.

Ballroom dancing was also a most necessary social attribute. During the Christmas holidays, having been firmly deposited by their parents at the Rotunda for this stage of their children's training in etiquette, two quivering groups of nervous adolescents, one male, one female, keeping as well-distanced from each other as possible, were forced to congregate for instruction in the intricacies of the veleta, the waltz, the gay gordons, and the Circassian circle. Once the excruciating fear of looking foolish abated, it was all jolly good fun. Life as a lady would be sadly barren and lacklustre if one could not familiarise oneself with the galloping exertion of the dosi-do and the quickstep, and one had to be adequately embellished with these social skills to impress the aristocratic young beaux at the hunt balls and society parties of one's future life – as the wife of a diplomat or a politician, maybe, or, simply, the County Lady from the Big House, who is a magistrate and is on the parish council and is a school governor and who reads *The Daily Telegraph* and *The Tatler, and The Daily Mail* when nobody is looking.

At any school, public or private, girls will be girls and do all the things that girls do, whether it be discussing the on-going physical development of their pre-pubescent bodies, or falling in love with the gym mistress, or chosen and revered prefects, or both. Our adolescent lusts and passions were no more ladylike or refined due to our attendance at such an establishment of gentility.

One of the advantages of a private education in those days was the opportunity you were given to travel. The pot of gold, once more, came to the fore. A month's stay in Scandinavia was arranged, which in those days was like going to the other side of the world. The boat train from Victoria took us down to Tilbury docks and thenceforth we embarked on to what looked like a very small vessel. She was called the *SS Patricia,* and was assigned to transport us across the North Sea. It was very rough. Everyone was seasick except myself, but the streets of Gothenburg took a long time to stop moving, when, with profound relief, we disembarked.

The first two weeks were spent camping in the northern mountains of Norway, staying in a remote log cabin. Every day, accompanied by our appointed instructors, we would climb the peaks. There would be a stop for lunch, to sample the delights of the smörgåsbord, and we were amazed at the variety of Scandinavian sweet breads – every flavour and spice, from coffee to cardamom.

Although mid summer, it was still very cold in this part of the northern hemisphere. We put on brave but shivering faces in our home made knitted jumpers, but our fearless Norwegian fellow climbers seemed unfairly immune to the subzero temperatures. They were also extraordinarily obsessed with cleanliness. In the cold claustrophobia of the log cabin, each girl would strip off twice a day for a thorough all-over cleansing, while we anglophiles were exceedingly reluctant to remove even one layer of our triple insulation. Our climbing friends must have thought us most unhygienic, as we gingerly took soap to blue and shaking body at much less frequent intervals.

Trekking up the mountains was exhilarating – strenuous, but invigorating and enjoyable, and a great sense of camaraderie developed between us all. We were young girls on an adventure, and any differences of culture and language faded into insignificance as we faced the physical and mental challenges of each new day. The shades and nuances of the light in this beautiful country were beguiling, and we understood very well why it was called the Land of the Midnight Sun.

For the second two weeks I stayed with my appointed 'exchange' girl and her family, who lived in southern Sweden, to learn something of Swedish family life. They were extremely hospitable, and living with them reinforced the view that Scandinavians were spotlessly clean, both in persons and home. You took your shoes off before entering the house, every surface gleamed, and any speck of dust was instantly removed. Bicycles were used whenever possible – they too were polished before and after use. Everyone was robustly fit and rudely healthy. They positively glowed with zest for life, and so did I.

The family owned a summer house on the shores of Lake Vanern, where they spent much of their time. We would swim and fish in the lake, build a fire, and cook fresh perch in the moonlight, sometimes staying the night and sleeping in a tent under the stars. I met some of their friends and learnt a little Swedish, and they were ever-keen to improve their skills in English speaking.

One of the purposes of the visit to the country was that the daughter of the house would have a return visit to stay with us in England. She would surely think us filthy in our rather grubby flat, but at least we no longer had a family of rodents sharing our home. She came, she saw, and with the bountiful and blonde stunning beauty enjoyed by young

Swedish womanhood, not only did she enjoy her trip, but she conquered quite a few young and lusty English hearts.

Before you left College you were required to attend Dr Browne's 'Talk to Leavers.' One was solemnly instructed to resist and preferably refrain from the temptations of the flesh and to lead a noble and upright life. How we lusty and hormone-driven schoolgirls smirked and revelled in the discomfiture of the blushing lecturer, who was, unfortunately for him, of the male gender. When I was about the age of twelve, my mother had, without being able to look me in the eye, slid a booklet into my hand entitled *Growing Up*, but we schoolgirls had, of course, learnt from each other what we needed to know well before then. We had also been presented with biology lessons about human reproduction from an equally florid-faced biology master, barely able to utter words as he struggled with his anguish and embarrassment. The subject of sex was never actually discussed with one's mother. In six years of attendance at the College, eight hundred or so girls per year, I remember only one instance of a young lady 'getting into trouble,' as the euphemism for pregnancy was in those innocent times. Nothing was actually said, but all the girls knew, and one day she just disappeared.

How were my parents able to send me to the Ladies' College? It transpires that in the 1850's Great-uncle Barnard, who was my grandmother's brother, and already quite comfortably off, made a very good investment by purchasing one of the best hotels in Penzance, just at the time when the great British seaside holiday became *'de rigueur'*, especially to the upper echelons of society.

Not only did the business prosper, but Great-uncle Barnard was businesslike and professional enough to ensure that shares and dividends were generously apportioned to all members of the immediate family, and an educational trust was also set up to provide private education for any children, or 'issue,' the term so-loved by the legal profession.

★ ★ ★

Part 3

*M*y mother was acutely aware that, in guiding her daughter in the art of social etiquette, and indeed in pursuing her own journey onward and upward through the ranks of social class, it was essential to meet people whom she considered to be acceptable.

She would take me to church nearly every Sunday. After the service, hat at a jaunty angle, she would frogmarch us both over to the vicar to ensure that we were noticed and spoken to. This social intercourse would surely lead to further contact and invitations? Among the various professional people she manipulated there seemed to be a penchant for vicars and doctors. I would then be forced to attend parties of their assorted offspring, not usually knowing any of them, and always with a strong aversion to being so manipulated. Protracted visits to Cavendish House would follow, in order to find the right fabric for yet another frock. In taffeta, cold and scratchy.

Enormous houses high-up in the rolling Cotswolds hills would be the ports of call, varying from vicarages and manor houses to mansions and farm houses, and usually filled with objets d'art of understated pedigree and taste. Wedgewood and Royal Doulton nestled nonchalantly on Chippendale dressers or Sheraton tables, Georgian silver gleamed gently from the tops of Steinways, portraits in oils of aristocratic ancestors adorned the William Morris extravagantly-papered walls, windows were draped with curtains of sumptuous rich velvets and lustrous damasks, and logs crackled beneath magnificent Adam mantelpieces.

Tiger skins were scattered about, so very dead looking, grim reminders of a beautiful beast brutally despatched, or the sad eyes of a shot stag stared at you from between huge antlers hanging from the walls. Fine Chinese carpets adorned the floors, threadbare and tatty, worth a fortune, everything generously layered with dust as well as the hair of dog and assorted other animals, and the pervading ambience was one of understated largesse and comfortably worn gentility.

Humble homes were notable by their absence, except for ours. Our old and battered but faithful Standard 10 lined up with the Daimlers, Bentleys, and expensive mud-caked shooting brakes at the appointed collection time for forcibly-partying daughters. The poor relation. All so embarrassing.

In spite of her eagerness to conform and to do as mothers do in the care of their daughters, my mother would have episodes when her attitude became irrationally volatile. She would be verbally very critical, inferring that I was far from bright, and many curses were cast forth at me for what seemed to be very minor transgressions. Often I felt there was no transgression. It was dispiriting and perplexing. No physical contact existed between my mother, my father, or myself, other than the occasional wallop from mother, – what a sad legacy from the strait-laced repressions of the Victorian era.

My father never joined in any social activities, with me, or my mother, except for the annual summer holiday. He would not go to any school function, or to church, or visit in hospital, or attend any public event. If a visitor came to the house, he would scurry away to another room. He was very odd in many ways. He was uncomfortable in the company of other people, but he was always willing to give me attention, to listen, and to give support and encouragement. I often wondered why he seemed to be so solitary. However, he unreservedly gave the affection and support which, for whatever reason, my mother seemed unable or unwilling to provide.

Despite the communication struggles we had between ourselves as a family, in many ways we lived a normal life and did normal things, even if not usually together. Friends were made at school. Françoise, as French and exotic as her name, was uncontrollably addicted to Fry's chocolate bars, but remained unfairly slim and chic. Beaky was thus named because her mother, Mrs. Beak, ran a chicken farm somewhere high up on a windy hill in the Cotswolds. It didn't seem humorous at the time.

My mother went to Paris. She brought me back a little white toy chow-chow and a red souvenir scarf covered with pictures of the Eiffel tower – an item she would, one day, as she exercised her continuing study of the upper classes mores, consider to be vulgar in the extreme. It did not occur to me at the time to wonder why she suddenly took flight to Paris, but it was odd.

We used to visit my father's parents every other Sunday, without fail. Before we owned a car the only mode of transport available was my father's B.S.A. motor bicycle, about which he greatly enthused and treated with great reverence. Riding it gave him power and masculinity and he loved it. My mother was inserted precariously into the side car for the bumpy journey from Cheltenham to Ross-on-Wye. She would sit grim-faced, hoping that none of her well-heeled friends or acquaintances would witness such an undignified spectacle. I would ride on the pillion, clinging onto my father's back. It was glorious fun, but hardly the appropriate vehicle for an embryonic Cheltenham lady.

Of my mother's family there was never any mention. We saw nobody and the matter was never mentioned. That was odd.

We once stayed in a caravan halfway up a mountain in North Wales. I was allowed to take my friend. She went to the grammar school, and didn't seem any the worse for it, in fact she seemed quite normal. It rained every day. Snowdon was lost in the mists of time. It was a holiday well forgotten.

Great-aunt Ethel, my grandmother's sister, owned a bungalow on the Norfolk Broads, and as it was offered rent-free to any of the family, it became an annual holiday destination for several years. On arrival, after a six hour cross-country drive in the bumpy Standard 10, with my mother's demeanour becoming increasingly irate with each mile, we were greeted by cackling geese at the farmhouse from whence we picked up the key. The property boasted cold running water only, and a primitive chemical lavatory, a convenience of unmitigated horror. Geese or the odd slimy and inquisitive rat or two would share the outdoor space. Home comforts were completely lacking.

To buy basic supplies you had to cross the water in a rickety punt. Like a ferry in the Dover straits, we would set off in a straight course, hoping for safe passage through the armada of enemy boats which zigzagged up and down and across. Our progress was slow, theirs was fast, and the amalgam of the two on water invariably equalled disaster, in collisions or near-misses. And, for us, one pint of milk too many could cause overload, causing both an undignified and unplanned exodus of punt-crew into the river and great merriment for the amused spectators.

Because this was a holiday, one assumed that hardships would be plentiful and the days stressful, but the compensations for discomforts lay in the variety of free entertainment offered by the misadventures of those individuals who should be prohibited from any water-bound activity, especially in a location as peaceful and tranquil as the Norfolk Broads. Great-aunt's bungalow was situated immediately on the river bank, presenting us with a bird's-eye view of any nautical episodes on the water, both expected and unexpected.

Hired yachts would tack up and down, usually skippered by young muscular men with Northern accents who sported little pompom hats, and with no experience of sailing a boat, who called the stern the 'back end,' and had no idea how greatly their raucous shrieks and laughs were magnified as they crossed the water, and how the moorhens scurried for cover in the reeds until the disturbance to their peace had passed. Often, mid-song and mid-confusion, and overladen with hilarity-inducing alcohol, they would collide with the wooden boarding at the river edge in front of our bungalow. The level of their intoxication, or lack of it, would then be detectable by their reactions and responses, which escalated from 'Very sorry Sir, my fault' at the polite bottom of the scale, proceeding to the top-end emission of wild and ungentlemanly expletives, generally directed at the skipper-in-charge of the offending boat, and a practised ignoring of our river frontage as they pretended not to see us.

Sometimes we would hire a motor boat and explore further afield, binoculars poised, to watch the bird and insect life in the reeds and on the water, from Hickling to Wroxham Broads, and beyond. We visited Great Yarmouth one day, as the patriotic British holiday-maker must, but my mother was less than impressed with the aura of fish and chips and abundance of kiss-me-quick hats, the sand was very forgettable, the grasses on the dunes scratched your feet, and the wind howled in from the cold and unfriendly North Sea.

We went to Potter Heigham where there was an exceptionally low bridge, and the skipper of any yacht had to lower his mast in order to pass underneath it. Invariably, the man at the stern of the vessel, responsible for guiding the boat through with a quant, would jam it into the river bed to propel his boat forward, the pole would stick in the mud, and the boat would sail on gracefully under the bridge, leaving him floundering, like a monkey on its greasy pole, before being tipped unceremoniously into the murky brown river, to the exuberant shouts of hysterical mirth from his nautical mates. My father thought this quite hilarious to watch, as it was.

The calm tranquility of the waters was always short-lived. My mother tolerated this holiday with stoicism of the highest order as there was little else on offer at the time. My father and I had great fun messing about with boats. He could be delightfully silly, and often managed to fall overboard. I think he did it on purpose to amuse us, and he did.

★ ★ ★

Part 4

*M*y mother was by now working full-time, and with my father often doing shift work, the care of their daughter became something of a problem in the school holidays. She was therefore frequently despatched to any friends or relatives willing or able to give her a roof over her head.

As a younger child, I had often been sent to my grandparents' home, usually by train, the guard given strict instructions to deliver me at the correct station. They lived an extraordinarily puritanical life, with few visitors, no radio, and barely any social life, so one's activities were limited. The main excitement of the day was the mile-long walk down to the town to buy a jam doughnut.

We would play a plethora of board games such as snakes and ladders and halma, but bagatelle was the most fun – the inverted horseshoe-shaped board would be set up in the kitchen beneath the hanging meat hooks, and with a satisfying 'twang' you shot your balls from a spring into a numbered pocket, hoping to accumulate a high score – far too infantile a pursuit for my grandfather, but as addictive as the amusement arcades of today. Knitted scarves grew and grew until they would have circumnavigated the town several times, and I constructed a flotilla of paper boats out of newspaper which sailed round the water butt and became the Spanish armada, but they enjoyed only a short battle before capsize and defeat.

My grandfather was a clerical gentleman, a vicar, a remote and academic figure, and my grandmother took the role of his subservient and dutiful wife, as was the custom of the time. While living in the same house, like my parents, they lived separate lives, joining forces only when the rules of social convention demanded. It was apparent that he considered my grandmother to be on something of a lesser intellectual plane to himself. He would reside in isolation, behind the desk in his study, and when we visited, every other Sunday, we would each be granted an audience with him, once on arrival, and again on departure. He always appeared serious and solemn – no humour, no frivolity, his Oxford-educated mind doubtless on matters of more intellectual consequence than a visit from his family.

My mother's time span always lasted the longest, suggesting that she must have achieved some sort of intellectual rapport with him, or maybe, notwithstanding his seriousness of mind, could it be that her youth, good looks, and inquisitiveness of mind sparked in him a response and interest not totally entirely suited to a man of the cloth? My father and I generally managed only a few minutes each, before, presumably, my grandfather's patience expired.

I remember him once quoting a section of *Gray's Elegy* to me, so we must have had occasional conversations. The point of the exercise was that you had to reconstitute the order of the vocabulary and phraseology in this particular quotation to create as many different meanings as was possible in the English language – an intellectual challenge which he must have deemed suitable for me at my age.

My grandparents employed a maid, customary in those days for most clergy, who were generally impoverished but eminently respectable. Annie performed all domestic duties, thus enabling them to coexist comfortably in their gentility. She 'lived in,' but was not permitted to use their lavatory, as she was a 'servant'. Thus in all weathers she had to venture forth to the bottom of the garden to use her privy, shared with the gardener, but, one hopes, not at the same time. There were numerous cupboards in the vicarage, stacked high with toilet paper, in case of another war. It was smooth and shiny, called *Bronco* and was not at all fit for its purpose.

Enormous joints of meat hung from kitchen ceiling, and the grandfather clock ticked away in the hall. In the winter paraffin stoves provided the only warmth, together with one open fireplace in the drawing-room, where the logs would crackle and spit. There were picnics under the walnut tree in the summer. Carpets of cowslips and buzzing of bees. Child on a tartan rug. Grown-ups in battered wicker chairs. Straw hats. Tea in a silver teapot, silver strainer removing the leaves. Muslin net over the milk jug, weighted down with coloured beads, to keep the insects out. Cucumber sandwiches. Wasps.

When my grandfather retired he and my grandmother moved to Herefordshire, and were thrust into a domestic situation totally unfamiliar to them. As their modest income from the Church was no longer forthcoming, they were unfortunately forced to look after themselves, facing the daily grind of housekeeping and catering.

Visiting on the never-changing alternate Sundays, the culinary offerings were depressingly limited and frugal. Sunday lunch consisted of a roast chicken, no gravy, served with bread and butter, no sign of a vegetable, a pot of tea to follow, and sugar lumps, extracted with silver sugar tongs from a silver bowl, both dull and tarnished now that Annie was not at hand with the silver polish. And chocolate mints – still a treat for us all after years of rationing.

My grandfather was eternally absent, always being at work in his study, but every evening my grandmother would dutifully and lovingly present him with a bowl of warm bread and milk. Every day, every year, no variables. She could not have cooked anything more challenging as she did not know how. Having enjoyed a privileged upbringing she thought it slightly demeaning for a lady in her position to have to apply her delicate hands to any matter of a domestic nature. However, the birds were fed daily, probably more nutritiously than the human beings.

My father had a fragile and strained relationship with my grandfather, and they struggled to be at ease with each other. As was the custom of the times, he had been sent away at the age of seven, thanks to his pot of gold, to a boarding school on the Isle of Wight. They behaved as two strangers, not with animosity, but due to the fact that they had spent so little time together, and because my grandfather had little idea how to relate to a child.

I was very fond of my grandmother. She was quiet, patient, and constantly kind. She had a strong Christian faith, and would diligently read her *Daily Light* and *Patience Strong* poems every day. I wear her engagement ring, and remember her with great affection.

Visits were organised for me to stay with Great-uncle Arthur, who was my grandfather's elder brother. He had been an architect of some eminence, and was married to Great-aunt Elsie, who was my godmother. They were both especially kind, perhaps as they had no children of their own, but they did have a cat called Susan which they adored. There was a disused Anderson shelter in their garden, a legacy from the war, which provided a womb-like and mysterious playhouse, becoming a different focus for the imagination every day. Aunt and Uncle would enjoy playing as well, and might visit one day to buy sweets when it was transformed into a shop, and another day would attend for a matinee performance of the dance. Uncle Arthur would read me a story every night, or sometimes a poem from Robert Louis Stevenson's *Child's Garden of Verses*. Aunt Elsie would always lay an extra place on the tea trolley in case of visitors, who never materialised. They had a lady called Mrs. Knight who 'did' for them.

The elder generation of our family in those days seemed to lead very sheltered lives, usually without transport, and tending to keep themselves to themselves, so, once again, the main daily activity was a walk down to the town to visit the shops. Aunt Elsie came to stay with us once. She always had a drip on the end of her nose.

Great-aunt Phyllis seemed to have mislaid her husband. We didn't see him and we never heard about him, but we knew he wasn't dead. They had two daughters, my father's cousins. They bred and showed dogs, winning copious quantities of rosettes and trophies at Crufts every year, as well as running boarding kennels, for all their eighty or so years. They could talk of little but matters canine, so we tended to give them a wide berth. We were of feline orientation.

I was sent with my cousin Malcolm to Uncle Bobby's apple farm in Essex for long periods in the holidays. Great-aunt Ethel, the owner of the holiday bungalow and one of my grandmother's sisters, used to lie on a chaise-longue most of the day, draped in voluminous scarves reminiscent of Isadora Duncan, communicating with the spirits of those who had gone before. She had always had people on hand who 'charred' for her, so had never needed to exert herself. Described by the family as 'delicate,' she reclined languidly in her gentile and privileged inertia until the age of ninety-two, constantly strong, robust, and indefatigable. She was always kind, as were all the aunts and uncles, but remote, as her mind was generally on a diverse spiritual plain somewhere else, unknown to us.

Predictably, in my family of strange but nice people, Aunt Ethel was yet another example, definitely odd and bordering on eccentric, but, thanks to the reserve of gold in the family educational pot, extremely well and expensively educated. Her husband Forster was for many years physically present but mentally absent, silently and contentedly. And odd.

The farm was a working farm, and covered quite a sizeable chunk of Essex with its extensive apple orchards, so people were always occupied with permanent activity and bustle, and the children tended to be left to their own devices. My cousin and I were therefore given free rein most days, being let out in the morning and usually retrieved at night. We played happily amongst the farm machinery, and tried to get the tools to work. We climbed trees, and fences, too high, too often. We explored the local ponds and streams searching for creatures to put in jars, and went too near the beehives.

I suppose we got fed but I don't remember it happening. Malcolm used to eat apples until he was ill. We bicycled every day, all over coastal Essex, and sometimes the twenty miles or so to the Yacht Club at Burnham-on-Crouch, where his sailing dinghy was moored. We sailed it around the Blackwater estuary and into the open sea more than once. Nobody knew where we were going. The navy-blazered and nautical-capped drinking fraternity in the bar of the Member's Club gave us some quizzical looks, but not an eyelid was batted. Foolhardy, undoubtedly, but to us it was an adventure of mammoth proportions.

I suppose someone 'kept an eye' on us. A governess was employed one summer, a healthy and exuberant Australian girl from Melbourne, but she did not seem to spend much time with us, our paths rarely crossing. Once we were allowed to stay out all night and sleep in an old gypsy caravan, owned by Aunt Ethel, and located in an isolated field near the dunes on the estuary. That time the governess was firmly instructed to remain with us at all times, and we were quite glad because the wind shrieked, the nights were black and starless, and the atmosphere was very eerie. Searchlights kept circling the coast and we thought we were going to be attacked by aliens.

Uncle Bobby was odd. He was a renowned lepidopterist. His whole life seemed to be spent in his 'bug house' which was sited in the centre of one of his fields, and lit with thousands of megawatts every night in the hope of attracting some interesting and hitherto undocumented specimen. He had researched and published several books on his subject and his depth of knowledge was greatly respected by anyone of note in the moth and butterfly world. When he made his visits to the British Museum he would be personally greeted by the Director and warmly welcomed into the inner sanctum of the establishment, a commendable accolade.

The most exciting thing about Uncle Bobby was that he kept a pony and trap, and would delight in driving it around the Essex lanes. Malcolm and I would sit at his side as he gathered all the straps and harnesses, and prepared to take to the road. We felt very important, not imagining many people were transported in such a splendour and graceful manner. The good-natured pony clip-clopped along obediently, and we hoped that he would not suddenly develop a spark of independence before cantering us into calamity. Over time, our fears proved ungrounded, but my uncle, wisely, never allowed either of us take control of the reins.

★ ★ ★

Part 5

*I*f the provision of child care by relatives in the holidays fell on stony ground, the remaining option for my parents was to keep me at home in Suffolk Square. When my father worked night shifts he would be in the house during the day. Sometimes, when he had days off, he would take me to motor cycle scrambles, with me riding pillion on the back of his bike. My mother would have been greatly agitated, had she known what was happening. She must have been out at work on these days. He really loved these events, and took great delight, in a rather masochistic way, in seeing the riders frequently get thrown off their machines. He would position us at the most perilous points of the circuit, as the engines roared and the mud flew, waiting for the excitement to begin. I had never seen him more animated.

We went walking up into the hills – perhaps to the Devil's Chimney on Leckhampton Hill, or on up to Cranham for a walk through the woods, or to Painswick to count the yews in the churchyard yet again, checking that there really were only ninety-nine. If we felt really energetic we would climb to the summit of Cleeve Hill, the highest point of the Cotswolds with an outstanding view, to let our eyes wander over the race course and the vista of Cheltenham, leading on to the blue-grey Malverns in the far distance, maybe enjoying a hard-boiled egg and a bottle of Tizer as we perched on our picnic rug. We took photographs, or 'snaps,' with a little box camera, and then would have to wait two weeks or more before the developed prints were returned, black and white, and very small.

I would sometimes catch the bus from Cheltenham to Gloucester. My mother's office was in the Shire Hall. We would have lunch and maybe spend some time in the cathedral. She would talk to me of the Three Choirs Festival, so trips to Worcester and Hereford were planned for one day in the future.

She was very fond of donning her best outfits and going out to eat, but exceedingly embarrassing company if standards were not met to an exemplary degree. Once she found part of a mouse's tail in her pudding. I can well remember the level of her explosive wrath, and how the whole restaurant, above Boots the Chemists in Cheltenham, was treated to the sound of her vocal tirade. Rightly so, if disgusted, but one can perhaps deal with such matters with quiet diplomacy. Not my mother. Not ever.

Every year, at the predicted time and on the high tide, we would generally drive to the banks of the river Severn to see the spectacle of the Bore. It was often cold, wet, and windy, but well worth the wait, as we watched the massive wave and the brave and sturdy souls who attempted to ride it.

On one occasion my mother took me to the Wild Fowl Trust at Slimbridge. I think she wanted to meet Peter Scott, as she so enjoyed dalliance with people of importance. We trudged our way through the acres of bird droppings and whirling feathers before reaching the Centre. Coincidentally, the man himself was indeed present that day, lecturing, and we did meet him. She must have known he would be there.

My mother would take me to London on the train – this in itself constituted an adventure. You stood in the corridor waiting to spot the Westbury White Horse, windows pulled down, smoke and smuts in your eyes. We used to stay in a seedy little hotel in Paddington. It was much too hot in the rooms and the pipes clanked all night.

She took me to the Festival of Britain on the South Bank, a magnificent symbol of celebration and hope for the future after the end of the Second World War. We admired the Festival Hall, the exciting Dome of Discovery awash with scientific innovations, the architectural wizardry of the tower named *Skylon* as it soared like a giant rocket into the heavens, the Big Dipper and the Big Wheel at the funfair, all of which dominated the London skyline.

My mother would dress very smartly for these expeditions, a tailored suit, generally in navy blue, classic and elegant, offset perhaps with one good piece of eye-catching jewellery, sometimes a stylish hat and a cheerful umbrella. Good shoes, good bag, every semblance of a lady. The perfect mother. Confident and assured, on a mission to broaden her child's horizons. She made all our clothes, from dressmaking patterns, Butterick and Style, bought, together with the fabrics – gingham and dayella or a good quality gabardine, from Cavendish House. Countless hours would then be spent hunched at her sewing machine, firstly with hands working overtime as she used her hand-driven model, and then advancing to a treadle-driven machine, when her feet would take over the furious whirring and clicking, and the pieces of material would steadily and miraculously metamorphose into garments.

This hive of industry disrupted life to quite an extent, as furniture was moved to allow space on the floor for the swathes of fabric. The numerous pieces of pattern, as fine and crumbly as tissue paper, were dissected and sorted and painstakingly pinned on to the material, as my mother, pins in mouth, wielding her scissors with consummate skill, crawled on all fours from piece to piece, cutting here, cutting there. Like a panther prowling round its young. Spools and threads and tapes everywhere. The real perplexity arrived, on completion of the cutting and pinning process, with the sorting of the paper pattern pieces and the impossible task of folding them in the correct sequence to allow successful reinsertion into their packets.

Social life was becoming more enjoyable, and I had made several good friends. The family had moved to a more acceptable flat, situated in one of the unattached houses immediately next to the church. It had originally been used as the servants' quarters of the house, which must have depressed my mother somewhat, but its saving grace was that, in its elevated position high over the Square, welcome beams of bright and unfamiliar light would filter through all the windows, except that of the bathroom, which faced, yes, a brick wall. But at least nobody could look in. The flat was still basic and lacking in the standards of the homes of most of my friends, so it remained very difficult to invite my friends home.

There never seemed to be anybody else in the flat other than the three of us, our nuclear trio. We had few visitors and struggled hard to present the correct image to the world. There was no garden, so, unbeknown to my mother and in our search for fresh air, my father and I would sometimes climb through a trapdoor in the larder to sit on the roof between the gables and the chimney tops. Just like chimney sweeps, without the brushes. All you could see was the roof of the church and the bird droppings, but it didn't matter, we had our own private place, and felt like naughty children together.

Compensation for lack of a garden was provided by the huge expanse of space in the Square. You could freely bicycle, play hopscotch, skip, and roller skate. It was our playground and a paradise of freedom. My friends and I energetically pursued our chosen activities, surrounded by the elite and gentile residents watching guardedly from their verandahs, as they delicately sipped their whiskies from cut glass, or their Earl Grey from bone china.

Childish things were put aside as the passage of time carried me from extreme youth to teenage, and it was important to show Cheltenham that I was also in training to be a Lady. Parading up and down the Promenade on a Saturday morning, chic, I thought, in a casually swinging trenchcoat, feet encased in daringly-high, but actually very low, heels. A little touch of Rimmel red on the lips, a subtle waft of L'Aimant, out to be seen, and maybe to succumb to the temptation of the wonderful shops. Eventually, the nearest coffee bar would be sought, usually near Neptune's fountain, and with aching toes and empty pockets I would watch the well-heeled and affluent Cheltonians perambulate purposefully past, heading for an interesting piece of art deco, or an antique vase, or a twinset from Jaeger, or a replacement item of school uniform for their child in Daniel Neals.

These trips to town took on even more significance in the school holidays, when the College boarders had returned to the parental fold, and we native-born residents satisfied the overwhelming need to reclaim our territorial rights, in taking to the streets of Cheltenham, our town, without having to compete for space with dozens of green girls who came forth from alien towns and villages to be educated.

I remember, at the age of fifteen or so, visiting my mother in Cheltenham hospital after she had undergone a routine operation. My father would not go. She had recently given me some cast-off shoes of hers – green latticed leather with a medium-high heel – rather dashing and higher than I had sported before. I wore them for the first time and felt incredibly mature with the added inches, and sauntered into the sterile post-anaesthetic atmosphere feeling like Ava Gardner, more concerned with the elegance of the shoes than the progress of my mother.

Parties were in ample supply. Young Farmers' Balls were bawdy and boisterous affairs, from which you needed a day or two to recover from the intense jollifications. Many a young farmer gave not of his best as he tended his livestock the following day, indeed he probably failed to remember the next day at all. Kenny Ball and his Jazzmen played at the Town Hall, for the Young Conservatives' Ball, which was a rather more salubrious and strait-laced event – more decorous, but where was the fun?

Boyfriends came and went. If I was allowed out in the evening my mother would always await my return home at curfew time of ten o'clock, alert as if on air raid duty and curtains twitching. Heaven forbid that you transgressed.

★ ★ ★

After these years of academic striving and learning, what was I to expect from the wide world and its opportunities, and what could I offer as my contribution? The newly hatched Cheltenham lady emerged, relatively unscathed, with a few good friends made during the rigours of the education process. What was she to do now? She was not particularly clever, had no heartfelt ambition or specific motivation, but was clean and tidy, pleasant and willing, and of good and optimistic disposition. The chrysalis had mutated to butterfly and was ready to spread its wings.

To fill the interval of indecision and temporary inertia my mother enrolled me at the local technical college for a course in what was then known as Domestic Science. It would always be useful, she said, and was right, as usual. The new environment of learning was very different to the formal environment of the Ladies' College, but it was refreshing to be working with students from all backgrounds, and it was useful to learn the traditional home-making skills. However, neither the ability to make choux pastry nor to starch a collar to stiff perfection was likely to thrust me into a promising career, or to make the world a better place.

And for the following year? Take a secretarial course – always useful, said my mother. She was right, again. It was enjoyable but hard work. Pitman's shorthand was taught, which took a year's worth of days to achieve the required standard, and endless restless nights spent with little hooks and lines careering confusedly round your brain. To learn typewriting we would sit at our electronic Silver Reeds day after day, fingers laboriously tapping the keys until the correct one was hit with the correct finger at the correct speed. Tuition in a mercifully less repetitive manner was provided by instruction in book-keeping and all aspects of business management.

Although we were treated kindly and professionally, we felt rather akin to monkeys or to Pavlov's dogs, trained to be on automatic transmission. It was all rather monotonous, but the method worked and it was useful to gain another certificate. And, as my mother had predicted, the skills would prove invaluable in the future.

★ ★ ★

Part 6

The time had come, as the Walrus said, to speak not of, in this case, sailing ships and sealing wax, but of things more immediately-concerning – to cease attending short time-filling training courses and to acquire a proper paid position of employment. My first job proved to be very undemanding, as a shorthand-typist in an office where you dealt with the ordering and delivering of coal, and all secretarial matters relating to the aforementioned coal. The coal-merchant-in-chief was the perfect image of Dickensian Uriah Heep, a dour man with a demeanour as black as the coal he sold. His other colleagues-in-coal were equally devoid of humour or lightness of heart, and there was nothing but relief when the time came to depart from this particular Slough of Despond. I can recall very little of this period, proving that the brain does, indeed, shut down on unwanted memories.

My next occupation was as a dental receptionist in a rather exclusive practice in Cheltenham, for a dentist who ran a very expensive car and a very expensive wife. He considered himself to be exceedingly grand. Having nothing more stimulating to do all day than to defer to his grandiose manner and to peer into the mouths of his condescending clientele, this position also proved to have short-lived appeal.

During this period of drifting rather aimlessly from one situation to another, my mother decided that enough was enough and her daughter should do something which would lead to a fulfilling career, something more in keeping with the ideals of Miss Beale. She therefore arranged an interview with the examining board for entry into the W.R.N.S., and

I was duly despatched by train to the recruiting office in Bristol. A naval entourage of stiffly-starched and uniformed female officers rigorously cross-examined me as to precisely why I wished to join this magnificent organisation in the service of our Queen, but as I could not pretend to have any sort of constructive or meaningful answer to this question it was no great surprise that the application was fairly rapidly refused.

'Let's at least get her driving,' said my mother. As she had, by now, acquired an extremely good job as Chief Civil Defence Officer of Gloucestershire, she had the useful advantage of knowing many of the great and the good in the area. Thus I found myself sitting, ashen-faced with fear, in a vehicle awaiting my first lesson from the recently-retired Chief Driving Examiner of the County, with instructions from my mother to get me through the Test. He had no mercy whatsoever, and the method he employed in giving his apprentice driver confidence in the presence of errant pedestrians was to bark in his broad Gloucestershire dialect 'Cattle! Cattle! Mow 'em down, mow 'em down!'

The aggressive approach succeeded, as the Test was passed with relative ease, probably because the relevant authorities were not a little afraid to fail anyone instructed by such a man of eminence in the world of driving tuition.

My father had already taught me the fundamentals of motoring, with patience of the highest order. He bought me a car – a Ford 8 model Y which had cost him the princely sum of sixty pounds. Modern for its day, it came complete with starting handle to wind it into obedience on a temperamental day, a running board to help you climb up into it, and a fan belt for which you had to carry spare stockings in the event of an emergency repair being required. Her maximum speed barely exceeded 50 m.p.h., and she never let me down on a journey. She might not always want to start, but once the engine was fired up and had burst into life she behaved impeccably. She would, however, rebel if threatened with any level road which suddenly metamorphosed into a steep hill. You had to either concede defeat and find another route, or, if in a fairly remote area, you could risk reversing up, horn blowing, praying wholeheartedly that no vehicle, tractor, horse, or person, was descending the hill at the same time. Going down was easy, as long as your brake cables remained intact.

Because he had such a mechanical mind, my father would constantly try to teach me how the engine worked, but his tuition fell on deaf ears. The attempted lesson always began as 'Imagine four jam jars', and then ground to a prescient halt due to my lack of interest. I knew in which aperture to place oil, water, and petrol, and where the starting handle was. What more did one need to know as a young lady who was unwilling to get her hands dirty? If necessary, you approached the nearest house or garage, playing the part of distressed damsel with twinkle of eye and as much charm as you could muster, and invariably help would then be volunteered, in the form of a strong and charming man with jack and wheel brace or battery charger at the ready.

Fate intervened. Glancing through *The Lady* magazine, I noticed an advertisement for a position as farm secretary at a dairy farm in Cornwall. It was summer, it sounded idyllic, and different. My mother was quite encouraging too, and together we drove the long way there, mainly in order that she could interview the farmers and establish whether or not they were good enough to take on her daughter. They passed her interrogation. I was offered the job.

My new employers proved to be affable and charming, and were to have a profound influence on the course of my future life. My mother had decided that, with her daughter now due to leave home, she had done her duty and could, with a clear conscience, abandon her miserable marriage and the nineteen years of living in silent and stoical forced cohabitation with someone to whom she was completely mismatched.

She left my father, on the same day that I departed for Cornwall. They were never to meet again. She gave me her new address. I asked her to look after my cat. My father was left in Suffolk Square, on his own.

On arrival at my new job I was, unsurprisingly, in a fragile state of mind. Though excited about the new job, I also felt confused and shocked at the sudden and sad situation left behind at home. As a child it never occurs to you that your parents might separate. You are too busy and self-absorbed to look too far outside yourself. Even if your heart tells you that things are not right, you put the matter aside and assume that things will always continue in the same old way. Unhappy and feeling very alone, I worried mainly about my father, and my cat, who had been, I'm ashamed to admit, more of a friend to me than my mother.

The farmer and his wife were very kind, understanding, and supportive, slipping into the role of *loco parentis*. He was a retired lieutenant-colonel from the Royal Scots, and his wife had enjoyed a long career with the Queen Alexandra's Royal Army Nursing Corps. They had both experienced years of outstanding service, both in peace and war, before retiring to this glorious location on the Rame peninsula west of Plymouth, to run a dairy farm and smallholding.

You were up at the crack of dawn for the first of the twice-daily milking sessions, together with a myriad of associated tasks. Whether driving a bone-rattling Ferguson tractor during hay-making, despatching countless finger-licking pots of cream by post, or talking nonsense to the Bambi-eyed creamy-brown Jersey cows, it was an idyllic way of life reminiscent of *Cider with Rosie* or *The Darling Buds of May*. Only Pop Larkin would have worked less and drunk more.

The colonel delivered vegetables and eggs once a week around the local village, with frequent stops for drinks and gossip with the inhabitants. This would take up most of the day, invariably ending up in one or more of the local hostelries. He taught me, by the rich hand of experience, the best of the local brews of beer, and how to survive the effects of overindulgence. You had to be capable of rising from your bed with aplomb the following morning, with no diminution of decorum and no detectable ill effects, and without in any way impeding the achievement of the milk quotas.

At times there would be a trip to the abattoir at Liskeard, with unwanted heifers on board the pick-up, happily unaware of their fate. This was an upsetting expedition, to me especially, so another trip to the pub was in order on the way home, to cheer us up.

The colonel was a hard taskmaster, and, in deference to his past distinguished army career, nothing less than the best performance in all activities would suffice. Standards were never allowed to slip.

My farming friends taught me much about life, and the values to which one should aspire, as they carried out their everyday activities in a simple, fulfilling, but quiet manner. Despite their financial standing, in no way obviously apparent, they treated everyone in like manner, with courtesy and kindness, and were consequentially greatly respected in the local community.

The farmer kept a hidden treasure in his barn – a magnificent Rolls Royce, a tangible reward for his years of hard work and service to Queen and Country. This was the only visible sign of his monetary wealth, emerging from its home between the hay bales only on rare occasions, when one dressed with an appropriate degree of elegance to enhance the beauty of the vehicle, perhaps to go to a wedding rather than a pig show. I was responsible for helping to clean it, with the greatest of care and a special silken duster. This exquisite machine was the jewel in the crown of motor cars, and, when sinking into the luxurious softness of the leather back seat, the degree of comfort could be compared with floating on a cloud, smooth, serene, silent, and stately.

One of the social highlights was the October visit to the big metropolis of London to visit both the Dairy Show and the Motor Show at Olympia, with an extravagant hotel stay in the West End. The Rolls came out of mothballs for its annual trip of any distance, and you felt you should be graciously extending your hand to the less privileged members of the populace, as you glided through the streets of London in such unbelievable grandeur.

The colonel's wife spoke to me in some depth of her nursing career, and he taught me about music. We used to sit in his summer house overlooking the hills, in theory writing some work-related letters, but in practice listening to Beethoven's Pastoral Symphony and gazing at the distant deep turquoise of the sea, head nodding, to sleep, perchance to dream.

They were both keen to guide me towards a useful future, and largely due to their influence I realised that I had to do something positive with my life to help other people, and so join a profession and become a State Registered Nurse.

Only the finest training would do, so I applied to the London Hospital in Whitechapel, now re-designated as the Royal London, because it was and still is known as one of the best centres of medical excellence in the world, with a long and famous history. With just enough qualifications under my belt to be considered, I was fortunate, not only to be granted an interview but also to be accepted on the next available course. My life ahead looked promising, and exciting, and, at last, had purpose.

It was several months before the hospital could offer me a place, so I obtained a temporary job at the Monkey Island Hotel in Bray-on-Thames, as a general help. This involved mainly domestic work, but also the serving of meals and waiting at table. You obtained a good insight into the process by which the average English male gradually loses his decorum and equilibrium as each successive glass of alcohol is consumed. The conference dinner was the biggest challenge – man without woman can, so often, become an uncivilised being.

Generally, couples behave, whether verbose or silent, but man alone with his fellow man will become an alter-ego, trying to impress his peers, and the larger the group, the more rapidly does the standard of behaviour decline into drunken abandonment. The situation provided regular practice in the cleaning up of regurgitated stomach contents, one of the more unappealing aspects of the career awaiting me.

★ ★ ★

Part 7

*T*raining to be a nurse in the nineteen-sixties was not for the faint-hearted, but the rewards and professional opportunities which lay ahead did provide a constant inducement to persevere and succeed.

The first stage was to report at the Preliminary Training School in the Bow Road, East London, for three months of intensive tuition, which was both academic and practical, culminating, if one had passed all the examinations, with visits to the hospital wards for practical experience. The regime was not dissimilar to army training, with strict discipline and unbendable rules, and a few students left, unable to cope with such restriction to their freedom. Every morning before breakfast you lined up before the Home Sister to be inspected, in matters of dress, demeanour and cleanliness of nails. We were taught the importance of a clean environment, and a newly-dusted surface would be checked by the Sister Tutor's white cloth. You did it again until not a speck was detectable. Visits home were restricted. Evenings out were not permitted, you were there to study. If you could survive these three months you had a fair chance of succeeding, and you were privileged to be training at the London Hospital.

We were young. We were strong. If you could get through this you could get through anything. We forged friendships, many of which would remain lifelong. We could laugh. We had to laugh. Some cried.

Once this period was completed, you started work at the main hospital. From the very first we were made to feel that it was an honour and a privilege to be working at such a famous and historic hospital, and if we served it well we would be appreciated and cared for. A strict code of etiquette prevailed, and we were taught to respect our seniors and defer to senior medical staff, but at no time were we treated as non-consequential members of staff, even when very junior.

How proud we were to be handed our smart new uniforms – in trendy mauve and white stripes, with distinctive leg-of-mutton sleeves – individually fitted and made for us from a design by Norman Hartnell. A fluted starched cap, which took much too much time to persuade into its pristine folds, and a crisp white fresh apron every day. Skirt no shorter than four inches below the knee, no jewellery, hair above the collar, shoes glowing. We were proud to look so professional.

When working on night duty you were expected to know the precise names and illnesses and treatments of each of your thirty or more patients by the time the Night Sister did her rounds at 10 p.m. You struggled to stay awake when bottle-feeding babies at four in the morning, eyelids drooping, starting to sway, but in mortal fear of dropping one's precious responsibility. You might be severely castigated by a draconian nursing sister, of which there were a few. But most were totally dedicated to their profession, had kind hearts, and would give praise and encouragement when it was deserved.

You saw appalling injuries, and inoperable retch-inducing cancers spreading mercilessly, but your feelings had to be suppressed, and you remained outwardly cheerful and giving of your best always, whatever the horrors before you. The endless time it could take for a patient to die seemed appalling, as was trying to find enough muscle in which to inject morphine, when all you could see and feel was skin and bone. Death could be all around you but you were taught to respect it as the final part of life – 'just imagine that this person was your own grandmother,' we would be told.

I remember vividly the first time I saw someone dead. The bell rang, and I was summoned to the ward. It was the middle of the night, quiet, dark, still, no hustle and bustle and light of the working day. The silence was oppressive. The ward was asleep. I saw the man, sitting bolt upright in his bed. It was his eyes I noticed first. He seemed to be staring straight at me, and as still as a statue, frozen in time. Was he, in his last throes of life, begging me for help, or was it that his eyes had seen their last, but retained their look of desperation in them? I stood looking at him, mesmerized, but nothing could make me touch him until I had called for assistance. I felt strangely privileged to be there, to be the first one to be with him, to show compassion, to do what had to be done, to witness and comprehend the extraordinary peace which death brings after a painful and distressing illness.

Industrial accidents occurred frequently, often in the nearby docklands, and were shocking every time. Grown men screamed with pain when their wounds were dressed, having perhaps succumbed to gas gangrene, or many others eventually died after suffering months of tortuous treatment for their extensive burns and severe injuries.

We all wanted to work on the men's orthopaedic ward which was, by comparison, as a bed of roses after a bed of thorns. Good cheer prevailed, with fit and virile young men on the wards who, though incapacitated in body, were generally not feeling ill, and were consequently rampant with masculine bravado and devilish in spirit, mischievous with the nurses but knowing where the boundaries were. Such camaraderie was uplifting for the patients' spirits, good for them and good for us.

Through all the time of working in this part of London, the spirit of the East End people was ever present. The local population then consisted largely of immigrant Jews, who often adopted the persona of the true Cockney, born within the sound of Bow Bells. They often struggled financially, many of them working as tailors in local family-run businesses, but they were intensely loyal to their families. They worshipped the nurses, were profoundly grateful to us when we cared for their kith and kin, and would inundate us with gifts and tokens of appreciation. We loved the affectionate way they talked to us when we spent time in the local markets and shops, and the special deals we could negotiate with the traders – 'Just for you, darlin'!' We bought jellied eels and cockles and mussels in the Whitechapel road, and on Sundays would wander round the market in Petticoat Lane, where you could buy a shirt for under a pound, only to take it home and discover that it didn't possess the sleeves it was supposed to have.

The aura of unease that eminated from historical times, like the spine-tingling tales of Jack the Ripper, would haunt us on troublesome days. As we walked through Whitechapel and Stepney and Brick Lane and past the Blind Beggar pub, where many devious plots of murder and horror were hatched, we were starkly reminded of the criminal and gangland culture of years gone by, and extremely relieved to be living a century later.

We learned about the life of Joseph Merrick, who had, in the late nineteenth century, been forced into a life of degradation and despair due to his severe and repugnant facial disfigurement. He became known as 'The Elephant Man'. Sir Frederick Treves, a distinguished surgeon at the hospital, took pity on him. Treating him with dignity and compassion, he gave Joseph a room on the upper floor of the hospital, and undertook to care for him for the rest of his life.

London in the nineteen-sixties was a magical city, the only place to be – it was a period of renaissance and excitement. The Sixties were apparently Swinging and we swung with them with all our energies. We worked very hard, we played very hard. We twisted the night away to the accompaniment of the mesmerizing songs of the Beatles, and we knew we looked irresistible in our flouncy skirts and Mary Quant dresses, usually bought in Carnaby Street, where 'flower power' ruled. Our mini-skirts were infinitesimally mini, but the thick black opaque tights which always adorned our legs afforded a satisfactory degree of modesty and decorum, and, it seemed, were very fetching to the male eye.

The hospital employed a secretary who oversaw our activities and 'kept a motherly eye' on us. She obtained theatre and museum tickets for us, organised holidays, and helped us get the most of living in the vibrant capital city. Every New Year we would join the massive crowds in Trafalgar Square to laugh and sing and be silly, to get soaked in the fountain, to bowl dustbin lids down Regent Street and to behave as a lady probably should not. We could do anything. And we laughed at almost anything. You had to.

The most prestigious highlight of my social calendar took place during the time of my training, not in London, but in Cambridge. A friend of mine from Cheltenham called – he had spent seven years at the Boys' College learning how to be a gentleman while I was at the Ladies' College learning how to be a lady – would I like to go with him to the Trinity College May Ball? How could one refuse?

Hot foot with anticipation, I set off for the Fens and a taste of undergraduate life, to spend a night of riotous and rigorous dancing, twisting to Chubby Checker or Elvis and smooching to Glenn Miller or Cole Porter, surrounded by the future leaders and thinkers of our country, most descending into the depths of debauchery as each hour passed. Would they, one wondered, make it till dawn, or would they slip gently and inexorably into unconsciousness, to recline in untidy heaps around the quads and the meadows, no longer capable of making philosophical pronouncements, or partying, or popping champagne corks, or putting their persons or their partners into a punt. Released from the mental application of their theses and their dissertations, for one glorious night they could, without a modicum of guilt, indulge in reckless profligacy.

My partner for the night had only been up a year, and was quite odd and shy. He had been working so hard that he had forgotten how to play, and had not yet become accustomed to the rigours of the customary heavy-drinking regime, ensuring that he remained upright into the cool dark hours of dawn.

Breakfast arrived for those of us still able to partake, and then, with heavy eyelids and feet which had energetically performed every dance-step taught at the Christmas holiday learning to dance for ladies classes at the Rotunda, and many which bore no description to anything, we folded ourselves unsteadily into our punt, to float dreamily and dopily through the meadows of the Cam, while the sun came up over King's College Chapel and suffused it with glorious golds and pinks. What a night.

Christmas was a special time. The doctors on duty would dress as fairies, adorned with garish make up and black fishnets, wings and wands, delivering gifts to patients and giving kisses to everybody, and to each other. The sisters would be dressed as angels, and would flirt outrageously with the fairies, and the rules were as relaxed as possible for the day. You got away with just about any wildness and silliness, as long as the patients' needs were the first consideration. There was a candlelit carol service in every ward, which was always very moving.

The hospital pantomime would be hilarious. A stuffy consultant by day would maybe stride the boards as a mad and generously-bosomed Widow Twanky, or a rigidly-starched and serious nursing sister would be reinvented as a lusciously long-legged Dick Whittington. We laughed till we cried.

In the second year of our training we moved to a brand-new residence, John Harrison House, the name of a past doctor of eminence. Each student had her own room and a bathroom shared between only two, which was new-found luxury for us. From the roof you had wonderful views of the London skyline, from the City to the docks, and much further afield on a clear day.

There were still occasional smogs at that time. The Clean-Air legislation of the fifties seemed not to have been obeyed to any extent by the industrial plants, factories and docklands of the East End. The atmosphere in the streets was intolerable, you could taste the filthy air as it reached your lungs, as well as it being a main cause of the prevailing high incidence of lung and chest diseases.

The area would become quite eerie and intimidating in fog, and your mind would wander back, yet again, to the times of Jack the Ripper, who had roamed the streets of Whitechapel only seventy years before, performing terrible and gruesome atrocities on women. The hairs on the back of your neck would stand up, as you imagined how it might have felt to suddenly hear footsteps behind you in the shadows, and you could almost sense his evil spirit in the swirling mists.

The presence of a fire escape at the home served us well, allowing re-entry after an illicit evening out, rather than providing an exit from fire. Curfew time was 10 p.m. You could get a late pass till midnight, not very satisfactory for lusty twenty-year-olds. The challenge was to evade detection. Romances came and went. We were all too busy and usually too tired to become serious about relationships, or commitment.

The work, academic and physical, was extremely hard, as were the long hours. We all had tough days when we thought we wanted to give up, but most of us kept going, supported by the encouragement of our families and colleagues. My saving grace was the uplifting correspondence which regularly reached my mail box from the colonel in Cornwall – always spurring me on with his interest and encouragement, and enclosing silly drawings and caricatures in his letters which made me laugh for the rest of the day. My father would often write, my mother only for birthdays.

I remember so well the night President John F. Kennedy was assassinated. We were putting on our best Carnaby Street frocks and party faces, preparing to go to the twenty-first birthday party of one of our colleagues. The news came over the radio. It seemed quite impossible to believe that such a charismatic figure on the world's political stage should suddenly no longer be with us, and the nature of his death had been so horrifying. The party went on, but one's thoughts kept wandering.

My mother was now living with John, who was to be her companion for the next twenty-five years, in a converted mill house between Warwick and Stratford-on-Avon. This had now become my family home, and I would periodically visit, but always at my instigation and never hers.

This was a temporary residence for them, as he eventually inherited a large estate in Sussex. She seemed to be very happy with him, and I was happy for her. I felt no rancour or bitterness towards her for leaving my father – what would have been the point, when faced with a fait accompli? With the passing of time, and with due reflection, I realised that for both their sakes, my parents' separation was inevitable. My angst was never about that, but about how she spoke to and treated me.

By now I had acquired a light grey Mini Minor – a generous twenty-first birthday gift. It became a faithful friend, and together the mini and I would circumnavigate the North Circular heading for

Warwickshire, and sometimes the long and winding road from East London to Cornwall to visit the farmers.

When my mother masterminded a first meeting for me and John one day in Stratford, he was very polite and pleasant – despite the difficult situation. He was Canadian, born to a well-to-do family and an only child, his father having died when he was but one year old. (Many years later, at his funeral, the aged vicar told the congregation that John's father had died a year before he was born – startling any somnolent listeners into somewhat amused perplexity.) Educated both in England and at Harvard, he had served in Burma during the war, and thus came from a more than adequately respectable background to please my mother, in her endless quest to ascend the social class ladder. He was also a very nice man.

When she knew I would be visiting, my mother would invariably organise tickets for the theatre at Stratford, where we attended some magnificent performances – Gielgud, Ralph Richardson (who was born in Cheltenham), Olivier, Flora Robson, Paul Robeson (an unforgettably powerful *Othello*) – and many of the greatest names of the English theatre. Country walks were also the order of the day, dog in tow. Along the river bank, sludge and mud, dog in, dog out, shaking and soaking all in its wake. Rural and relaxed, this pace of life was a soothing antithesis to the pressures of the working environment.

My mother and John did not seem to mix much with friends or neighbours while I was there. Friends, or even acquaintances, were sparse in number, and as my mother always chose to live at a suitably superior distance from other people there were seldom any neighbours to meet – they were endowed with a touch of the Squire-and-Lady demeanour even then. On one occasion, when I was afflicted with tonsillitis, my mother called out the local lady doctor who duly arrived at full canter on horseback, ruddy of complexion and gangly of gait, complete with medical equipment rattling in the black bag on the heaving hindquarters of her trusted steed. I thought she might gallop back with antibiotics, but no. We had to gallop to the chemist in the car.

Sometimes we went a little further afield. The new Coventry

cathedral was uplifting to the soul, as it towered over the ruins of the original building destroyed in the bombing raids of the Second World War, a magnificent triumph of good over evil. Graham Sutherland's acclaimed tapestry of Christ, however, was difficult to appreciate – modern art perhaps, but so different to one's traditional pre-conceived ideas of how He should be portrayed.

My mother was now the proud owner of a Triumph Spitfire coupé – a sleek and sexy low-slung beauty, not unlike her. She had always been a frightening driver as she was too vain to wear spectacles, but despite having a few near misses she had always managed to avoid death, hers, mine, or anyone else's, and cut a fine figure of a woman at the wheel of this stylish maiden. Quite incredibly, she occasionally allowed me to drive it. This came a close second to floating silently in luxurious leather in the rear of the Rolls Royce. I found many reasons to suddenly go into town, and, please may I borrow the car?

These years were maybe the smoothest in our problematic and perplexing mother-daughter relationship. I was unattached, working hard and enjoying life to the full, she was very happy with John and they were both still working. There was no time to ponder. I had not yet upset the applecart, but it wouldn't be long before I did.

However it was still impossible to feel comfortable and relaxed with each other.

★ ★ ★

Part 8

*A*s nursing students in the Sixties we did not have a great deal of free time, but we took every opportunity to enjoy life to the full. All the attractions of the capital were within an easy bus or tube journey – museums and galleries, theatre and cinema. In hot weather we would go to Victoria park, or take a bus down to Epping to walk in the forest, or plunge into the hospital swimming pool, which, miraculously, could be covered over to become a tennis court for the winter months.

We needed holidays to help us through the stresses of our work. The nearest local seaside resort was Southend-on-Sea, but with the cheap package holiday industry rapidly expanding and growing in popularity, a visit there held limited appeal. We all wanted to see something of foreign lands, and, as full-time students, were offered remarkably low fares on all forms of travel, which we exploited to the full.

A group of us went to Ireland, beginning with a few nights in Dublin – we could only afford a few – at the Sheraton Hotel, in supreme style. Having explored the city, and visited the Guinness factory tour and tasted its end-product – which was deeply-brown and creamy-topped and delicious – we then trekked down the east coast, as lazily as the gently-swaying and unsociably-scented donkeys with their carts. They were always driven by a friendly Paddy O'Mara, and would, sadly, soon be disturbed by the rude invasion of man's essential accessory – the motor car. Miles and miles of white sand, hardly a person in sight, total peace and pleasure.

I had always wanted to visit Italy. One of my fellow travellers lived in Chelsea, in a fine eighteenth century house in Cheyne Walk. Her parents were bohemian and hippy, and everyone called them by their Christian names, even their children. How odd. I stayed with them the night before we departed. It took an age to draw off a few inches of tepid bath water fuelled by the sad little Ascot wall heater, allowing ample time to admire the intricately stuccoed ceilings as one shivered.

We took the train, staying awake as long as possible while France flashed before us, to eventually collapse, exhausted, into our couchettes to slumber through the lengthy journey. Our holiday home was a small 'pensione' near Rimini on the Adriatic coast, and we revelled in the freedom, breathing in the sun, the sea, the magic. Every night the chattering Italians – 'padre', 'madre', with their many 'bambini'- would wander the streets and sing of *'amore'*, and drink, and dance, in love with life. My friends and I fell under the spell.

It had always been an ambition to visit Venice. Neither parent had ever shown any particular interest in art, but from some unknown source a reproduction of the doge's palace by Canaletto had materialised, which had hung splendidly over the mantelpiece in the drawing room of our humble flat in Suffolk Square, and it had made a profound impression on me.

I was not disappointed – it was a unique city, unlike any other. Our essential gondola trip carried us, swaying precariously, through the dank and malodorous canals and under the mysterious Bridge of Sighs, where, so rumour has it, if you kiss your lover at sunset your love will endure. Back on dry land, through the piazzas, over the Rialto bridge, and to the magnificent Basilica and St. Mark's Square, which was packed with too many people and pigeons, and photographers. We bought 'gelato' from beautiful Italian men with huge brown heart-stopping eyes, and soaked in the atmosphere, in more ways than one – Venice is a more than a little pungent on bad days.

The whistle-stop coach tour took us on to Florence. From the foothills of the Apennines you suddenly came upon a vast panorama of architectural masterpieces, like glowing jewels alongside the lazy Arno, with the vast Duomo cathedral casting its massive shadows across the city, and on to the Uffizi, the world's pinnacle of art galleries.

The Medici collection was quite overpowering in its beauty and magnitude and colours. You could not possibly absorb every nuance of every great painting. Had we really been so close to the work of the masters – Leonardo, a genius at everything, Botticelli, Michelangelo – the fulsome voluptuousness of Titian's Venus, and the Reynolds who had painted the picture of the little boy with a rabbit which had hung over your bed. Time was too short. It was like trying to eat a traditional Christmas dinner in twenty minutes, and the intensity of cultural concentration was waning.

As we returned to our bus, sinking into our seats exhausted but elated, I remember returning to trivial girlish thoughts. I wondered quite how my travelling companion managed to re-apply her lipstick so deftly without the aid of a mirror. A beautiful girl needing no artificial aids, she was also a delight to be with because she had no idea how beautiful she was – 'bellissimo!', gasped the young Italian studs. And why had my grandmother been named 'Florence'? Had her wealthy Victorian parents followed their forefathers and done the 'Grand Tour' and been as impressed with it as we had been?

A rail trip to Scotland was another adventure. Steaming off on the overnight sleeper, arriving bleary-eyed the following morning in Edinburgh, a few days were spent absorbing the atmosphere and history of this historic city, then some window shopping in Princes Street, and the long ascent of Arthur's Mount, with wonderful views over the city and beyond. Back on board the train we gently travelled up the west coast, stopping briefly in Glasgow, which we could not leave quickly enough – drab, dirty, soulless. Then on to Oban, culminating with the incredibly beautiful trip to the fishing port of Mallaig, purported, rightly so, to be one of the great railway journeys in the world. We were transported effortlessly on as far north as Inverness before making our way back down the rugged and beautiful east coast.

I remember the Saturday morning when our final examination results came through, and after three years of hard work, I was at last entitled to wear the hospital badge and call myself a State Registered Nurse, entitled to add three important letters after my name.

In my euphoria, I had forgotten how difficult things could

sometimes be with my mother. I telephoned to pass on my good news, but her dismissive response and lack of interest was dispiriting. She, of course had wanted me to be at least a doctor, so no words of congratulation were forthcoming. Four years of hard slog endured, and not one word of praise. The glass always seemed to be half empty rather than half full where her daughter was concerned.

Mother was an enigma. She would buy me expensive presents, sheepskin coats, garnets and pearls, leather bags, and of course my wonderful mini, but this largesse did little to assuage the hurt inflicted because of her attitude. Why couldn't she relate to her daughter in a normal way? My brain would buzz with frustration – was she off-loading guilt by her material extravagance towards me, did she think it made her a good mother? Whereas she seemed to sometimes treat her maternal role with gravitas and a heavy semblance of barely-disguised duty, she would also be content to ignore it for long periods of time. Never being invited to go and visit them still hurt; I always had to make the first move, and I had the impression she did not actually like me very much. She could not accept me as I was – but only as her rather disappointing daughter, reminding her of a past which she had obliterated from her mind. A few bricks would be optimistically placed on the tower, only for them to be knocked off again soon after.

In those halcyon days of job opportunity and security of employment, once qualified one was automatically offered a post as Staff Nurse, if you wished to stay on at the hospital.

A year working in the private wing of the hospital followed, which was fairly uneventful, but offered the interest and challenge of meeting people from all over the world, who had come to this famous hospital in London for the best medical care in the world that money could buy.

It was time to move on. Two fellow graduates and I applied to study midwifery in Plymouth, a gruelling course. Many patients unbelievably ignorant about basic human anatomy. Nine months after the last large naval vessel had sailed a goodly number of young women would be admitted to the maternity ward, with the birth of their babies imminent. They often had very little knowledge or understanding as to how they had become pregnant, or of what childbirth was all about, having been too inebriated at the time to remember.

Childbirth and labour on a daily basis proved to have limited appeal. Joy was too close to tragedy. There were graphic memories – a twelve-year-old girl struggling to give birth, as every scream of pain ripped any remaining shred of childhood from within her – the look on the face of a beautiful young woman who, following a massive haemorrhage, had to undergo the swift action of a surgeon's knife, removing her womb to save her life, and the turmoil of grief and relief in her husband – and the young lady who lay calmly on her bed reading magazines and knitting while she produced her baby, without a murmur. Extraordinary.

The professional and social restrictions of this period, compared with London life, were only relieved by the making of some more very good friends, and the beautiful countryside and coast around us. The Red Light district of Union Street and wandering the docks was not for us. And I had met a nice man shortly before starting the course. I was missing him.

A colleague and I experienced one unforgettable day when we could forget about midwifery, escaping to a world to which all young ladies of breeding aspired to enter. Her mother knew someone who knew someone who managed to obtain tickets for the Royal Enclosure at Royal Ascot. We hired our hats and dressed in our best frocks and headed for the Shires. We inscribed counterfeit badges to announce that we were 'Lady-this' and 'Lady-that', raised our voices a few decibels to aristocratic levels, clipped our vowels to upper-class intensity, and consumed a little too much of the generously-flowing champagne.

The cunning plan must have worked, as we were treated by the very important people in the Enclosure with the appropriate level of reverence due to two titled ladies of impeccable heritage. Except that neither of us were. The activities with the horses were comparatively unimportant. This expedition was a social event par excellence in this six-month period of toil and trouble, a highlight of great enjoyment and slight deceit.

Most of us completed the course and were able to proudly add more letters after our names.

★ ★ ★

Part 9

*B*y now, in my mid-twenties, marriage was beckoning. Henry and I had first met in London, when he was introduced to me by one of my colleagues as a 'blind date', being the son of a friend of her mother's, and he was duly designated to be my partner at one of the very grand hospital balls at the Grosvenor Hotel. He went to great lengths to organise his dinner jacket and dashingly striped trousers to perfection, no small task when you rise six feet and six inches upwards into the stratosphere. We had a wonderful evening, and the seeds of friendship were sown with elegance and humour.

While he was teaching in west London and I was in Plymouth, we had frequently travelled up and down the A303, and it was so good to have a pleasant and reliable friend when feeling so geographically isolated in the far west.

Henry proposed to me one night after a mackerel and beer supper, high up on a cliff top overlooking the lights of Plymouth Sound, the Eddystone lighthouse flashing encouragement in the far distance. The stars twinkled, life was good, and it certainly seemed to be a very good idea. In our euphoria, we had temporarily forgotten our combined mothers.

My mother vehemently opposed both engagement and the planned wedding. This was an inauspicious beginning, and the subject of matrimony was going to undermine our relationship, which had never been brilliant. Apparently I was throwing my life away, and losing the independence needed to reach the top of my profession. This rendered me unworthy of discussion among her class-ridden and status-obsessed friends. She was, surely, taking Miss Beale's example of a dedicated career a little too much to heart, and yet heart seemed to be what was lacking.

Determined to be heard, and obeyed, she and John drove the long way from east Sussex to Plymouth and to take me out to lunch at the best hotel in a desperate attempt to dissuade me from going ahead with the marriage. This, of course only increased my dogged determination to proceed.

Eventually she deferred to the inevitable, conceded defeat, and gave us her reluctant blessing. The wedding went ahead in Windsor, with my mother doing her elegantly-clad best to do the right thing, in an atmosphere which was racked with false good cheer and bonhomie. Mother-in-law too was a considerable force to be reckoned with, and our combined mothers glared at each other over the wedding feast with mutual suspicion and distrust, vying with each other to detect lapses of good taste, in dress, speech, or manners.

With hope in our hearts and the eternal optimism of youth Henry and I embarked on the new adventure called marriage. It was not easy, it never is. We lived according to the stereotypical pattern of the time, with the husband going out to work to support his family and the wife perhaps taking on part-time work until a family came along, but responsible for all domestic matters and house-keeping. I had no resentment towards this concept because that was how marriage was perceived to work at the time, unless one could afford domestic help.

Our first house was a little semi-detached in the Home Counties. We were happy living there, but when my mother made her one and only visit to us, to deliver my old cat whom she had housed during my years of study, she remarked, ironically, with a sad lack of humour, that there was hardly room to swing a cat. But it was our home, and we were content enough.

My faithful grey mini had now been replaced with a Morris Minor, in a fashionable deep aubergine hue, which happily matched most outfits. It oozed character, and offered a safe and secure feeling in your womb-like capsule of English engineering at its very best and most

Florence and David, circa 1918

Walter, Florence and David, circa 1925

Grace and Heather, 1963

Robert and Edmund, 1972

From 3…

… to 53

Granddaughter Belle, 2004

reliable. The upholstery was soft leather and the bright orange indicators would shoot out obediently from either side, like arrows from a bow. It was as solid as a tank, the steering was hard work, and you could not reach any significant speed, but it was a faithful friend for several years.

The position of Staff Nurse at the local hospital lasted for a few years, before a spell as Nursing Officer for the local Red Cross Society. I had been volunteered by a well-meaning friend, for in truth they had no one else available to ask at the time. There were meetings to attend and training in first aid to be given. Then, as no one else was prepared to take it on, a period as commandant followed. This was an honorary position, sounding rather pompous, but it mainly involved acting as a figure head at civic functions, and laying a poppy wreath on Remembrance Day at the war memorial on cold November days. You met a large and interesting cross-section of society, and it was a useful and fulfilling form of voluntary work.

Henry and I each had our own friends and interests, and life was busy and hectic for us both.

'Let's go to the National Cat Show,' said my cat-loving friend, 'and bring your cat.' So one dismal dawn we set out from a still-slumbering suburbia to Olympia, the back seat of her car layered with six assorted caged cats – five of hers, one of mine. The show was in full flow when we arrived, and the noise was unbearable, an all-pervading and overwhelming cacophony of human cackle and feline protestations pitched at ear-torturing decibel levels. We duly reported in, signed the requisite forms, deposited the animals in the delegated penned areas, and jostled for position with cat people from all corners of the country to view the exhibits and to talk cat talk, and to buy cat things. There was nothing but cat.

Most of the judges were, as most of their kin are, a breed apart – sensible shoes, pleated Harris tweed skirts, jumpers and waistcoats, clipboards in hands, that unmistakable air of perceived self-importance. They cruised along the aisles, eager and earnest, whiskers a-twitch, stopping at each cage to analyse the physical attributes of claw, jaw, and paw, before making their final and crucial decisions, to eventually award the much-sought-after trophies to the honoured moggies and their ecstatic owners.

Our cat, of a very high Siamese pedigree with a long unpronounceable Siamese name, was called Jason by us. He treated the day out with the greatest disdain. He had never been to a cat show before, and he never wished to do so again. He knew he was a top cat, he did not need to be told, and without any trouble to himself, had walked away from Olympia with two Championship awards, two certificates, and two very smart rosettes. He hadn't even tried.

Henry and I visited friends and family. One of them was Great-aunt Mollie, who had also benefited from the pot of gold, and after a very expensive education had become a geologist. She, like most of the family, was a little odd. She married an equally odd homeopath who practised varying forms of quackery, which he called alternative medicine, on unsuspecting but satisfactorily rich patients. They resided at an expensive address in West London, overlooking a handsome Georgian square, until he decided to abandon his matrimonial responsibilities to go off with his secretary, leaving Great-aunt with no children but an exceedingly raucous minah bird called George. We looked after it for her once. It strained our nerves to distraction with its unwholesome cage to clean and its constant shriek of 'Hallo George', which was the name of the errant and misbehaving husband.

Great-aunt Mollie was my second godmother, and for sixty years she never failed to write at Christmas and birthdays. She left me a little of her pot of gold when she died, in the form of a gold watch and bracelet.

My husband was very well connected in the musical world. Not only did he introduce me to the works of many and varied composers, but had access to complimentary tickets for any of the Henry Wood promenade concerts that we wished to attend. So of course we did, and often. We listened to world famous orchestras and performers, directed by notable conductors, musical showmen of their time like Boult, Barbirolli, Beecham, and Sargant. Dressed in our black ties and long evening dresses, sipping the best champagne and feeling profoundly important as we sat in the grandeur of a box, we looked downwards towards the less-fortunates who were relegated to stalls and circle.

They were memorable evenings, but most vividly remembered are the performances which had a 'hitch' – like the night when a string broke with a resounding 'twang' on Jacqueline du Pre's cello, a problem she calmly fixed, to continue with her hauntingly evocative and beautiful rendition of Elgar's concerto – surely the definitive performance to this day?

When in the middle of the rousing sounds of Walton's Belshazzar's Feast the famous baritone collapsed on to the podium, overcome by the ever-present stifling heat of the Albert Hall, the performance was saved from disaster by a young music student who appeared in the wings and offered to take over. He had recently been studying the work, was word and note perfect, and received a finely-deserved standing ovation when he took his bow, resplendent in his jeans and T-shirt.

Settling down for one concert, we discovered that we were sitting next to the great soprano Dame Eva Turner. This was a trifle intimidating until she turned round, and in the broad lilt of her native Lancashire, offered us sweets from a paper bag on her lap, and embarked on a friendly chat about which were the best toffees to buy and how her shoes were a little tight.

I remember the speech given by Sir Malcolm Sargent on what was to be his final 'Last Night of the Proms.' He was by then extremely ill, his hair still sleekly brylcreemed, the ever-present red carnation in his buttonhole, dapper but dying. He was filled with morphine. A doctor was waiting in the wings in case of need, and nobody knew whether or not he would manage to get through it. He did. It was very moving. Three weeks later he was dead.

I was fortunate, and content with life. Henry and I worked hard, but had many good times, visits to friends, and regular holidays – these never quite seemed to live up to expectations.

One visit to the depths of the Scottish highlands, was during an unseasonably cold late August – the wind blew and the rain dripped, and we wondered why we were there. But the British spirit prevailed. Loch Lomond was vast and cold and there was no sign of the monster. Shivering, we donned our lightweight summer macs and tramped through the wet bracken and up the hills. Even the soaring flights of falcons and hawks were absent. The greatest and most eagerly anticipated daily pleasure was the return to a roaring log-fire at our excellent hostelry. The joys of Scotland did not inspire us as they did Robbie Burns, extolling its virtues in braes and burns, and waxing lyrically to his poetic paramours.

Another holiday on the Spanish Costa Brava sounded so appealing in the brochure, as is always the case, but there were far too many British en masse, determined to remain stoically English, unwilling to be courteous to the country they were visiting by trying to speak a few Spanish words, or tasting a little of their native cuisine, or learning something of their culture. But we enjoyed the sun and the warm sea and our last real holiday as just a couple.

The time came to have a family and we were fortunate in having two fine boys, Robert and Edmund, within four years of each other. I gave up full-time work, as you did at that time. We both threw ourselves enthusiastically into our newly-acquired roles as parents.

My husband worked away from home a great deal, but it was on our behalf, and what everyone did those days. At times I felt that it would have been good for us as a family if he could have spent more time with me and the boys, but studying and earning a living had to take priority, which I understood. I was happy to be at home full-time while raising the children, as every day presented such delights and challenges as they grew and developed into individual characters.

My husband, had also been an only child and was only seven when his father died. He had been brought up by two forceful women, his mother and grandmother, who, together, formed a considerable challenge to our marriage. But, as long as one trod carefully and their dear boy was happy, all remained well and they were united in their delight when the children arrived. We visited Henry's mother regularly, spending holidays in her seaside home, and the two little boys brought much joy to a loving grandmother.

I had optimistically assumed that the arrival of grandchildren just might be the catalyst which would miraculously transform my mother into a different persona, possibly resulting in an improvement in our relationship. Perhaps she would be able to enjoy being a grandmother – indeed, how could it be that a woman would not to want to get to know her own grandchildren? My heart hoped that she would take a real interest in them, but my brain told me that this would be unlikely. They were too much part of me, her daughter, too alien a part of my life for her, so how could she suddenly develop any normal feeling towards them? She had no time or patience for the silliness and joys of young children, yet she had spent many years in Cheltenham giving of her time with socially deprived teenagers. But they belonged to someone else, she was not expected to become close to them, so she could keep any emotions firmly locked away – the teacher and social worker rather than mother or grandmother. I had no illusions; I knew, sadly, my children would never know real love or affection from the woman who was my mother.

She and John had now taken over the Big House and Estate in Sussex, ironically named 'The Cottage.' From the minor country road, the entrance drive seemed endless – such was its exclusivity; the huge expanse of lawn was dominated by a flagpole – an indication of gracious living on the grandest scale. The grounds vast, the rooms extensive, and much of the inherited furniture was antique, French, worth a fortune. Some of the paintings would have happily graced the walls of the Tate in London or the Uffizi in Florence, and the sale of the centuries-old ticking grandfather clocks in their lustrous mahogany cases would have financed several terms of a private education.

As time went on, my mother metamorphosed into the role of 'grande dame.' The well-heeled country set she associated with seemed to be of one ilk, loud of voice and superior in manner, so it didn't take long before she too assumed these characteristics, almost as though she had been rehearsing for the part. Her voice became increasingly fortissimo and staccato, as her haughty air became more intimidating.

She and John were happy managing the house and maintaining the extensive grounds and woodland, involving themselves in village affairs as and when necessary, and living the hunting, shooting, and fishing life of the affluent country dweller. They ran the obligatory estate car and labrador, wore shabby green waxed jackets and muddy green wellingtons, carried shooting sticks with panache, attended Country Fairs and County Shows, and talked to the right sort of people. They fished for salmon on Deeside in Scotland, and visited John's cousins in Canada.

My mother would remark on how the Canadians judged people by who they were and what they had achieved in life, rather than by their background. Had I been more astute, this might have been the time to tentatively ask about hers. But the book of secrets had always been kept firmly closed, with no information about her absent family ever tendered. Whatever the issues concerned, they were private, locked up deep within herself, not to be probed. Knowing this one kept one's counsel, and I was much too frightened of her to tread such a very dangerous path.

John was quiet and charming, a gentleman born, with no delusions of grandeur. He knew how to handle my mother's affectations, and was the only person to whom she would actually listen. He had inherited a vast fortune through an ancestor who had been a master silversmith in London, who, with a fellow-craftsman, had produced quality pieces of such high calibre that their reputation quickly grew.

The excellence of the silversmith's work had been brought to the attention of King George the Third, with the result that he and his associate were commissioned to provide the Court with silver, and were appointed by the king to be royal silversmiths. It appears that the king was sometimes short of cash and would rather settle his bills in kind, with items of immense value from the royal house. The fortune grew for the silversmiths on Ludgate Hill, and over the years it escalated into another very sizeable pot of gold.

My mother did the right thing by congratulating me when the children arrived. However, in all her years of grand-parenthood she never addressed them by name, or showed any real interest in them. She ignored my husband's existence. For years she would send a Christmas card addressed to me and the boys, always excluding his name. Not once did she invite us to go and visit them.

This situation both distressed and disturbed me, it was so abnormal

– such a difficult one to live with, to come to terms with, or to rectify. I felt embarrassed because of my husband's understandable disdain for her, and to a degree my loyalty had to be with him. He would have nothing to do with her – why should I? Because I was her daughter. I believe I had done my utmost to treat her as one should treat one's mother, whatever one's inner feelings, but I was baffled, confused, and close to admitting defeat. Robert and Edmund seemed unaffected by the absence of this grandmother, – still too young to ask questions, and they had the devotion of their other 'Granny'.

This, sadly, was the time when a period of almost total estrangement began, as my mother's disinterest, bordering on disapproval, became apparent. My husband, understandably, had no wish to communicate with her, so any visits and overtures had to be of my doing alone. She obviously did not wish to lose all connection with us, because birthday and Christmas cards were still exchanged. The cord was not completely severed.

As the children grew older, with a dragging and wavering conscience, I did occasionally gather them and myself forth, and venture again to Sussex, heavy of heart. It was all so difficult, and it shouldn't have been. My mother did not mistreat the boys in any way, she simply had no real interest in them. Her voice and manner were as overpowering and dominating as ever, I quivered with fear. I would not be defeated. Fortunately the boys, at their young ages, did not seem too aware of the odd situation, but in later years they must have wondered about it.

All was not lost – muster stations would be called and preparations made for the regulatory dog walk On one occasion all was well until we returned towards the house, taking the normal route which passed the entrance to the Bluebell Line railway. A queue of people had formed, awaiting admission. In her loudest fortissimo my mother announced that we could not possibly go past the 'peasants', so a detour was made. Her perceived importance in her role as the Lady of the House was quite extraordinary. Very ironic, when I eventually discovered something of her family roots.

John was a soul of diplomacy, constantly endeavouring to ease the difficulties and atmosphere of froideur between mother and daughter. I was very fond of him, he'd always been very kind, and we had a good relationship, but as my mother and I became increasingly estranged, this relationship too had become more tenuous.

Other storm clouds were on the horizon. Insidiously and irretrievably Henry and I were experiencing difficulties with our marriage, so hard to understand and confront, so numbing for the mind and spirit. There wasn't even any real animosity, just an emptiness, a nothing where there should have been a something. We struggled on, every day an agony of miserable indecision, finally coming to the painful realisation that we would probably be happier apart than together.

Henry remained in London. I decided to return to my native and much-loved West Country. Our elder son lived with me, and the younger one with him, not an ideal situation but the one which suited us all best at the time. Each child saw each parent regularly, and we always kept in touch, with the welfare of both boys being of paramount importance.

Eventually we divorced, and I felt I owed it to my mother to tell her. She offered to give me money if needed. I thanked her very much but declined her offer. I did wonder whether her attitude would change now that I was unattached, but it didn't, and she made no comment about what had happened.

My father was sorry that we were to separate, but was supportive and non judgmental. He and Henry had mutual respect for one another, and would continue to correspond until my father died.

★ ★ ★

Part 10

*A*new life lay ahead, in a small market town in Somerset. I would be independent once more, with the challenge of building a new life and career, with my son's welfare being the most important consideration. Henry had, very reasonably, helped me finance the house, so for economic reasons I had to find a job, quickly. There were debts to pay.

I was offered a post as Staff Nurse at the community hospital in town, which was small, friendly, and served the local populace very well. The job was varied, and no two days were alike. The pay was good, and the work rewarding.

My mother telephoned me one evening; uniquely this had never happened before, and asked for my father's address, as she needed to write to him. It was surprising, but I wasn't overly concerned, and only learnt of the reason a few months later. She wrote to me the following Christmas to inform me that John had died in September. I had not even known that he was ill. She had needed to contact my father in order to initiate divorce proceedings, so she could marry John and thus legitimise her inheritance. As she did not tell me of his death when it happened I had no opportunity to show my respects by attending the funeral. I found this very difficult to understand.

Always believing the philosophy that education should be an ongoing part of life, I knuckled down to advanced classes in sociology and psychology. Would the study of Freud, and other renowned psychologists give me an insight into why my mother found it so hard to look me in the eye? Or address me by my name, or want to visit us? Freud might have theorised that her behaviour was a form of defence mechanism – was she repressing or denying emotions because they were too threatening to her, or unconsciously modelling herself upon another person's character and behaviour in order to suppress inner conflicts and insecurities? That sounded very probable. Maybe she was not treated kindly as a child, and the pattern was being repeated as her resentment simmered below the surface.

The boys were growing and would be leaving home soon, to follow their studies and make their own contributions to the world. Despite their father and I going our separate ways, they had both grown into self-assured and well balanced young men, both, thankfully, with a healthy sense of humour and lightness of heart. Robert, showing remarkable aptitude for all things technological and already with a higher diploma in electrical engineering, was leaving for Manchester and a course in sound engineering, and Edmund had won a place at Cambridge.

New friendships were made and nurtured. Long-standing friends were valued, and came to visit. We would explore the local beauty spots. I acquired a dog called Samantha from the local animal rescue centre, a collie-cross with a placid and affectionate temperament, and she helped me meet other like-minded people who had dogs and enjoyed walking and the countryside. We would tramp the towpaths from Bradford-on-Avon to Bath along the Kennet and Avon canal, and along disused railways lines through woods reeking with the wonderful aroma of wild garlic, all over Wiltshire and Somerset.

There were organised walking holidays, like the one to the Lake District, where the rain came down like glass rods every day, and Lake Coniston could barely be detected through the unforgiving sheet of water. This adventurous pursuit proved to be suitable for only the most hardy and hearty walker, because even a purpose-built Barbour raincoat did not prevent the freezing dribbles of water eventually descending down one's back, like cold and slimy snakes. At that point the nature of the expedition changes abruptly from pleasure to ordeal, but, because you are on holiday, you remember you are British, grit your chattering teeth, force your mouth into a grim smile, and will your sodden and struggling feet determinedly onwards through the squelching quagmires ahead. To be a professionally-equipped walker you also have to buy proper walking boots, invariably very expensive and very uncomfortable – too tight with socks on and too loose with socks off. The final accompaniment is a knapsack on your back, which is heavy and difficult to reach, so you have to stop, only to discover that it, too, is wet, and so is your packed lunch. Nevertheless, despite the physical discomforts, one met many people from all over the world, and the camaraderie and pleasure of finding new friends made the holiday very enjoyable.

Another week was spent in Charmouth, from where we explored Chesil Beach and the Jurassic coastline, looking for, and finding, fossils, to then visit the museum to delve into their ages and history. It was hot and lovely. And dry. No water, except in the sea, and in the taps.

Independence was good, fortunately having good health, loyal colleagues and fun-loving friends. By this time my father had moved to be nearer me and his eldest grandson – he was always wonderful company, and was a frequent visitor. But I missed male company. Life as a singleton has its limitations, particularly when attending social occasions such as dinner parties, and on holidays. Perhaps a dating agency would come up with the perfect companion? This courageous diversion into unknown territory produced some pleasant encounters, and some less so.

Speeding along the auto-routes of France, imprisoned in the rear of a fast and erratic vehicle belonging to one of these candidates, and feeling nauseous due to continuous plumes of noxious fumes permeating from the chain-smoking front-seat occupants, I decided that this episode would be the last. There would be no more seeking a partner by artificial means. Matters did not bode well, given that the day before we were due to depart on this potentially romantic break, he had announced that his daughter was coming too, I didn't mind did I? Not only this, but she, too, was a chain smoker. *Quelle horreur!*

Having looked forward with enthusiasm to the three-week holiday with my partner-booked-through-an-agency, it was soon apparent that mutual stoicism would be needed in no small measure, as I disappeared for yet another solitary day with books, baguette, vin blanc, and sketch pad, and my companion left for the nearest town and the *supermarché*, arm-in-arm with his personable but father-fixated daughter.

A misguided adventure! Whatever would be would be, and life was quite full and active enough for the time being, without the vagaries of the male gender upsetting one's equilibrium.

I was not unhappy with my own company. My house was on the edge of town, bordering open countryside, and overlooking the railway line, maybe ordinary, but easy to look after, with a beautiful flowering cherry tree in the front garden, not as imposing as a flagpole, but good enough for me.

Life was going well, and my small Somerset town was a pleasant place to live, and was close enough to Bath and Bristol to satisfy any sudden cravings for culture. There was a splendid view over the fields and hills to distant Longleat House. Sometimes the managers of the estate would promote special events, such as ballooning, and I would watch the enormous canopies arise out of the morning mist, baskets swinging precariously underneath, looking like brightly coloured light bulbs as they hissed and puffed through the clear blue and pink sky, gliding gently and gracefully over the acres of conifers way beneath them.

The back garden led down to the shrubland alongside the railway, with the regular trains emitting a comforting roar as they sped past the back of the house. The expresses shot through like bullets, people barely detectable at the windows, and the quarry wagons took forever, juddering past with their gigantic loads of stone recently excavated from the depths of the Mendip hills. You could set your clocks by the whooshes and the rumbles. Thus there was always unlimited excitement for any visiting child, or, in truth, adult, who was enthusiastic about railways.

Bird life was abundant, and rabbits would scurry over the lines, putting their furry little bodies at risk of immediate extermination by the next Penzance to Paddington express. The cats would regularly tantalise the field mice, and kestrels, hawks, and buzzards never went hungry.

By now, the job was becoming stressful, with too much bureaucracy creeping into the workplace. Time once spent looking after patients now had to be spent doing paperwork. Targets and budgets became the raison d'être of the working day. The 'nanny state' was rearing its ugly head, and decision making was being taken away. A triple-written directive was required to get a light bulb replaced. You no longer had any autonomy. Common sense was being eroded, people could no longer be themselves, or enjoy job satisfaction.

The time had come for a change, and I was offered the position of Nursing Sister in a private nursing home, a fifteen-minute drive from home across the Deverill hills. It was worth taking the job for the commute alone, passing as it did through glorious countryside where the sheep safely grazed and rapeseed turned the fields to a vividly-blinding yellow, like acres of custard, and through the middle of the valley the Wylye river meandered gently past the back gardens of the pretty thatched cottages, like a slithering silver snake. In autumn the scarlets and reds and golds of the acers and beeches were as remarkable as any you would see in Maine or Vermont.

The work was most enjoyable, and the home very well run by a Matron and team of staff who strived to give the best possible care to their residents. Of course the work was physically hard, but invariably rewarding, and many of the residents had interesting tales to tell about their past lives.

Our visiting architect, overseeing further building work on the site, provided regular entertainment. His name was Jack, a charming man, with a charming wife and charming children. We enthusiastically looked forward to the returns from his holidays, when he would regale us at the luncheon table with extraordinary amusing tales. Any venture outside these shores would attract unplanned disaster.

He and his family went to the south of France to find their rented cottage double-booked, and occupied by two women, one sweet and feminine, one heavy and hirsute, giving every indication of being in love with each other and thoroughly inebriated with a generous smattering of drink and drugs. Too tired to fight this Gorgon and her friend for their rights, they squeezed into their car for the night. Having eventually found alternative accommodation, they endured two weeks of storms, before getting lost on their way home, somewhere between Dover and Hampshire.

Always believing that things must get better, for their next holiday they embarked on a canal boat trip to enjoy some peace and tranquility. Jack succeeded, with an unbelievable profusion of navigational errors, to completely block the canal when he tried to turn the boat around. A nautical tail-back of all other craft ensued, and the helpful men from the Waterways Board had to be contacted to extricate him from his embarrassing predicament. He may well have been able to solve the problem on paper to the finest degree of accuracy, but the practical solution eluded him. Protractor and technical drawing-board, yes, but road map and driving-the-boat, no. What fun we had listening to him, and he was just as amused at his misfortunes as we were.

We did work hard between these welcome interludes of entertainment and excellent lunches, and after two years, with an aching back brought on by constant lifting of heavy patients, I approached the Manager's office. With a twinkle in the eye and not a hint of seriousness in the request, I asked him whether he could offer me a relaxed and comfortable sitting-down job anywhere. The gods were with me. I became his personal assistant and within another year or so assumed responsibility for the business and financial administration of the nursing home.

With my own office, and the 'go-ahead' to choose my own curtains and re-arrange the furniture, this felt like the entrée to a serious management role, and in the years to come this would turn out to be both personally and professionally fulfilling.

★ ★ ★

Part 11

*I*did not meet the man I was to marry until I was nearly fifty, and certainly hadn't been actively seeking a husband. My former manager owned an apartment in France near Montpellier, and he kept on talking about his friend, who had been on holiday there with him. I took scant notice, concentrating at the time on budget controls and projections on expenditure, but as the talk went on and on about James, his name seeming to infiltrate into every conversation.

Inevitably James and I eventually met, and two years later we were married in a small village in Wiltshire. I invited my mother, feeling honour-bound to do so. Unsurprisingly, she made an excuse for her absence. My father had never attended any social function in his life so I didn't bother to ask him. However several members of the family and good friends attended, ensuring that it was a happy occasion.

We bought an old cottage in the village that had been on the market for two years because it was so dilapidated and run-down that nobody wanted to touch it. The price had therefore dropped, but the potential of the property was obvious. My husband knew he could overcome all its problems, and the following years were spent happily working on the project, as well as continuing with our normal jobs.

A stone outhouse in the garden was transformed into a holiday cottage which we could rent out to visitors. Before being permitted to open to the public, a South West Tourist Board inspection took place, to ensure that all standards were met to its satisfaction. A gentleman named Caspar (who could possibly christen their child thus?) duly arrived on the doorstep, his remit being to inspect the cottage. He was very charming, but the 'small talk' soon ebbed to reveal the intrinsic nature of his visit, and the challenge of his day appeared to be 'grouting.' He was on a mission to detect grouting of a substandard nature. There could have been rats at the back door and a boiler in danger of imminent explosion, but still it seemed that the grouting was the only matter worthy of serious consideration and assessment.

The condition of our aforementioned grouting must have passed muster, satisfactorily uncontaminated by surfeits of unfriendly microorganisms, because Caspar's inspection resulted in the award of a coveted three stars on the certificate, which proclaimed that our cottage was a suitable habitation for the general public. Our standards were beyond reproach. It felt like winning an Oscar.

Albert and Sheila were due to come over from New Zealand to stay in the cottage for three months, and when Albert telephoned to confirm arrangements he had sounded like an energetic and worldly traveller of, perhaps, middle years. When we opened the door to greet them our hearts trembled. They were both well into their eighties, and both looked reasonably unlikely to remain on this mortal coil for the allotted time span. Albert just looked old, but Sheila was very deaf, rattled with medication, and had a tendency to fall over at regular intervals.

However, after they had spent a few days settling in, it was clear no physical problem would defeat either of them, and the level of their energies knew no bounds. Every day they would be up early, sprightly and earnest, and venturing forth on family or cultural pursuits, returning late in the afternoon to gratefully pick up the fresh vegetables we would leave at their back door. One of their many interests was the study of crop circles. Armed with their assorted pills, potions, ordnance survey maps, geological surveys, and the latest scientific papers on the naturalistic and paranormal theories for the causes of these phenomena, they would disappear into the wilds of the Wiltshire fields for the day, as happy as a sand boy and girl, but bound instead for mud and long grass.

We were sorry to see Albert and Sheila leave, back home to their much missed cat and their bungalow in the beautiful North Island, from where they could gaze towards the South Pacific, and dream of the history, culture, and the crop circles in the British Isles which they so loved and we could call our "*sceptered isle, our precious stone set in a silver sea.*"

James and I enjoyed travelling. France, especially, held many attractions for us both, and memories are many and vivid – not merely the predictable images of awe-inspiring cathedrals, mighty winding rivers, pure white sands on beaches which never end, and warm waters of blue perfection – but those, also, of real life.

An *assiette de fruit de mer* piled high with every possible crustacean from the deep Atlantic, fresh and succulent and awaiting your messy dissection, as you draped copious napkin around your neck and approached your prey, armed with assorted culinary implements that looked more attuned to radical surgery on an operating table, and then to messily scrabble and wrestle with claw and tool in your quest to detach every tasty morsel of magnificence and transfer it successfully from plate to mouth.

Standing armpit-to-armpit in a rickety little single-decker bus heading from Montpellier to the cool fresh air and sea of the Mediterranean, when the city was so hot and sultry that it was impossible to stay there during the heat of the day – hot and glowing, as ladies do, rather than vulgar sweating, and in bone-rattling transportation, every day for a sweltering week, we suffered this test of endurance in anticipation of the relief ahead. The ancient vehicle burst with an assorted mass of hot humanity, each of whom hung on to the overhead straps and chattered loudly enough to break glass, as the garrulous driver, entering avidly into the general bonhomie, smoked and swung his perilous route round every French corner and pothole he could find.

Trying to avoid being accosted by Madame Graniér, who lived next-door to our rented apartment in the Limousin, was a daily challenge. Every time we left or returned to our temporary abode, her door would quiver and open a crack, and out she would jump, exploding like a brand-new Jack-in-the-box, wound up and ready to go. Trapped again.

A twenty-minute expostulation in her language would ensue, expelled from her lips with such speed that it was impossible to understand the content of the conversation, or to offer a sensible response. We would intersperse *'Oui'* with *'Non'* in desperation. But we were English, and owed it to our country to work at some semblance of entente cordiale. We passed her door silently, trying to avoid touching the old squeaky French floor boards, we almost stopped breathing, we prayed for deliverance, but to no avail.

I had a cousin who lived in Paris, in an apartment which lurked in the depths of Montmartre. Reggie would meet us at nine in the morning, eager and ready to absorb the amusements of the day, and cajole us into the nearest café for his first pastis.

Vibrating with joie de vivre, he was passionate about living in such a bustling and vibrant area of the city, which exuded the ambience of the Impressionists art movement of the eighteen-sixties. For a painter such as Manet, who was a revolutionary in his depiction of female nudity on canvas and a hero of the young radicals, it was in one of these cafés that he would meet his fellow artists such as Renoir and Degas, to drink, to discuss their work and to debate. Here we were now, sipping our café noir, every space on the wall ablaze with colourful reproduction prints of the great masters, and you could well imagine how the café buzzed with life, then as now – the sense of perpetuity was almost tangible.

Reggie had lived in his top-floor paradise for years, overlooking the artists' quarter, first with a wife, and then without a wife when she tired of his preference for alcohol over her. He knew all the local artists, artisans, and intelligentsia, and was tête-à-tête with the most hospitable hoteliers and bartenders of the area. In his chosen establishment of the day, he would join the assembled gathering, rampant with bonhomie. Any transient visitors to Paris would also be heartily welcomed and encouraged to enjoy the pleasure of his company. He would introduce them to everyone, and, as a speaker of fluent French, would also enjoy acting as an unofficial translator, so could advise them how to inform the hotelier that cold water ran from their hot tap or that they had seen a mouse in their bedroom.

Having perused *La Monde* briefly while still relatively sober, the wine would begin to flow, the increasingly garrulous conversation, in whichever language, would become louder and sillier, and eventually beyond comprehension. The resident matriarch would sit unperturbed at the rear of the café – core of the family, revered and respected, *la grand-mère,* cigarette in mouth, skinning a rabbit or feeding a dog or two.

Life, according to Reggie, was meant to be enjoyed, but interspersed at very regular intervals with liberal eating and drinking. Very often, having escaped from these lively and loud interludes in the café and the exhaustion of his magnetic personality, we would escape to the peace and quiet of the nearest garden or gallery, and meet up later for an excellent *plat de jour* and probably more alcohol.

At night, as darkness fell in the Rue des Martyrs, garage doors would discreetly open to reveal, not a car, but the seedy side of life in Paris. Hulky brutish transvestites, adorned in their flashy dresses and with lips luscious and gleaming, would appear on the street eager to attract those of similarly weird orientation. Bewigged and bewitching, high heels tottering precariously on the cobbles of Montmartre, scented and sensuous, how entertaining it was to behold such theatre. How my husband blanched for fear of being propositioned!

We enjoyed the 'bateau-mouche' boat trips on the Seine, as every conscientious visitor must, with the Japanese avidly photographing anything which moved, including taking continuous shots of their friends taking photographs.

The extraordinary Pompidou Centre was similar to a child's meccano set, or a giant inverted central-heating system, an unforgiving tangle of pipes and metal in vivid reds, whites, and blues. The breathtaking view from the top of the Montparnasse tower dwarfed the Eiffel tower in the far distance. The lift rocketed you up to the top in seconds, leaving your stomach at ground level.

We lazed in the indolence of a picnic by the river with baguette, Roquefort and a bottle of fine vintage red. There was no other city in the world which could infuse you with atmosphere, in quite the same way as Paris.

The magnificence of Sacre Coeur, with its spectacular view across the city, even more so at night. The Louvre. The Left Bank. The gardens. Notre Dame. The cemeteries, the tombs, Rodin's great work of art *The Kiss* — time to reflect and time to feel — the inborn courtesy of the French — *'Bonjour'* and *'Au Revoir'* and *'Madame'*, always.

Dear Reggie. We were so fond of him. He immortalised Paris for us. Sadly he is no longer with us — too much pastis and red wine, too often, for too long.

★ ★ ★

Part 12

J ames came from such a normal family. His parents lived contentedly together, getting on in years, but companionable and devoted to one another. They loved their children and grandchildren. We would often visit for Sunday lunch, or they would come to us. His relatives seemed to have married and stayed married, and had two or three children – not the lonely singletons who seemed to be peculiar to my odd family. They regarded it as their duty to care for each other if they were ill or suffering the frailties of age.

To me this example of family life was a revelation, and a reassurance that I could get on very well with everyone except my mother – the problem had to be with her. I'd felt immediately at ease and welcomed by my new 'in-laws' – he a quiet and dependable man, happiest in his garden growing every variety of flower and vegetable, and she a kindhearted country woman, worldly-wise and astute through her experience of people and life. She would telephone on a Sunday simply to enquire as to how we were. She even used to ask me how my children were, though she didn't really know them. Normal questions and answers, normal interest, talking and listening, exchanges of opinions and ideas, being comfortably in one another's company.

It was therefore almost incomprehensible to James that there could be such difficulties in a family as I experienced with my mother, as it was a situation outside his experience.

James struck an immediate rapport with my father, who was an easy going and gentle man, but meeting my mother presented more of a challenge. I had tried to explain how the impasse in our relationship had come about. Impartial and sensible, he considered as we were all getting older, together we should make an attempt to face the apparent blockage in communication by going to see her, and by trying to understand and resolve the problems. He had no axe to grind, and with an open and pleasant manner would surely accommodate anyone. He had mixed with all levels of society and had no inhibitions or fears about meeting my mother. His mind was open.

Plucking up courage which I didn't have, I picked up the telephone. I suggested we visited her, and a date was arranged. She did not converse normally on the telephone. Each short response would be monosyllabic and barked, rather than spoken. This encounter was going to be as intimidating as I had feared. She never succeeded in sounding as if she wanted to see you, but was too well-mannered to refuse or to make excuses. However she agreed to meet us.

She'd now moved from the great estate to another house in Sussex. It was a smaller residence, but with a very large garden and part of a wood, and was remotely situated, as befitting a wealthy widow who did not wish to be living too near her fellow man, or woman. Ever eager to give the right impression to her remote neighbours and very occasional visitors, she seemed to now consider herself to be even grander than when John was alive.

'Turn left at the vulgar pub, and look for the weather vane,' were the instructions for locating the new house. We searched, to no avail. Eventually we found we were approaching familiar-looking territory, we had seen it all before, another massive lawn, another flagpole, this must be it, almost as imposing as 'The Cottage' had been. Straight out of the pages of *Country Homes,* this house had originally been used as a brickyard, and was now, after much renovation, a traditional Sussex cottage in warm-red brick, with a few outhouses – indeed a solidly-conservative desirable property in a very conservative area. Rayburn and dog were present but, sadly, no John.

Introductions were brisk and correct. Drinks were offered. She and James shared the same tipple, and she had always related more easily to men than to women. She was in her element. They got on. This wasn't too bad. She held court, always liking to be the centre of attention, and seemed to be at guarded ease with me. You did not speak, nor were you listened to, you were talked at. We were shown over the house and then the garden, together with a lemon tree in the greenhouse, a source of great pride. She asked after 'the boys' but paid scant attention to my reply, showing no further real interest. There were no family photographs to be seen in the house, except one of herself and John taken a week before he died.

A walk was taken with the dog in the Ashdown forest. She encouraged James to drive her car – and appeared to enjoy having the company of a man again. She was fit, and cheerfully-equipped with wellingtons and walking stick, led the way with enthusiasm. She walked the dog in the Ashdown Forest every day. We asked her if she did not feel vulnerable in this isolated house, especially when alone at night. Despite having security lights, her nearest neighbours would be unlikely to see or hear any disturbance. She told us she has a shotgun under her bed and would not hesitate to use it should it be necessary. 'Go for the knee,' she said, 'that way you won't kill 'em.' I have no doubt that she would have taken aim and fired, if faced with an intruder.

The visit was over. Although the distance between us was hard to overcome, and the atmosphere was uncomfortably formal, especially for myself, we had survived. No further damage had been caused. The impasse was broken. We had crossed the Rubicon.

A fragile pattern of contact followed. Although we were still never actually invited to the house, we would initiate a visit at regular if infrequent intervals. Invariably they would include one at about the time of her birthday – exactly one week before mine. She would greet us quite warmly, insisting we came to lunch, and went to a great deal of effort to entertain in the grand manner – perhaps we'd be served a whole salmon, caught by herself. Napkins starched to military precision, silver gleaming, we sat to attention, rigid-backed and obedient. Fortunately one had been taught one's table manners.

Conversation was formal and stilted, silences were protracted and painful, although we were all trying desperately hard to sound relaxed. But social convention prevailed, and she would cross-examine us briefly about our current activities, but, as usual, did not really pay heed to our responses. So, in stultified discomfiture, one listened rather than spoke.

I wished she would ask me about her grandsons, but she rarely did. It saddened me deeply. They were doing so well, and an ordinary grandmother would have so loved to take an interest and have some contact with them. Robert had proved himself to be something of a social entrepreneur, having set up a global educational networking internet site for underprivileged youngsters, as well as designing websites for major companies. Edmund, having followed a distinguished academic path and gaining a doctorate in economics in Belgium, was now working for the Central European Bank in Brussels.

The strange situation with their grandmother had never seemed to bother either of my sons unduly and they had not asked questions. But I always felt that, through no fault of their own, they had been cheated of something important. I liked to think that, with wisdom beyond their years, they had realised that with the fragile unpredictability of human relationships, there were occasions when the total of two and two, however entered into the calculation, was never going to make four.

Sometimes she would take us to the nearest Country House Hotel, where the great and the good of the local gentry would congregate and talk in loud and patronising voices, eyeing any whom they considered to be their social inferiors with mild disdain. Again we would sit to attention as my mother held the stage. She had always enjoyed playing to an audience. I often felt she was on the stage at the Old Vic, acting the role of a lifetime. Who was she really, beneath the veneer and her play-acting?

Our times in Sussex became something of a ritual. We would firstly be shown round the garden and grounds which she so loved, the first port of call always being the greenhouse and the lemon tree. This had become, to me, perhaps a symbol of hope, because it offered a welcome subject of interest and more relaxed discussion. It was something we could admire and share, something to bring us together. She bought us one at Christmas. We looked after her tree when she died. It never bore fruit for us.

I was beginning to realise that my relationship with my mother, although on the surface improving marginally, was never going to intrinsically change – too much time had passed; she was the person she was, and, indeed, I was the person I was. She could never get close to anyone because she would never let her guard down enough to be honest and to speak openly.

There was only one person who had stayed in touch with my mother from her 'past life' – Jane, who had been her secretary in Gloucester. Jane had experienced various problems in her own family, and my mother had 'taken her under her wing' and had been a loyal source of support and help to her. Jane was just a few years older than I was, and, although unaware of it at the time, I unconsciously felt as if my mother was transferring the care and concern which she could not feel for me to Jane. Jane had also, ironically, become the mother of two boys, and they would be welcomed to my mother's house, and taken on fishing trips with John when he was alive. When I discovered this, I felt the acuteness of our rift, and sad that this kind of family involvement did not happen for us.

Jane had spent far more time with my mother over the years than I did, and used to visit her regularly. They had a sort of strong rapport borne out of the shared experiences in the many years they had known each other. Jane and I got on very well, and she, too, admitted to me that, although fond of my mother, my mother had often belittled her, making her feel inadequate and childlike. Other acquaintances, too, would admit to me that they usually felt totally intimidated by her.

In many ways these tales brought me a sense of relief – it was, I hoped, not my fault that this relationship had been so laboured, because I assumed my deficiencies and frailties were no greater than those of any normal human being, and what is normal? Maybe I had expected too much all along.

My mother went on many and various cruises with one or two of her wealthy friends. She would tell us about her latest trip. Although she would often have little idea of exactly where she had been, she would recount hilarious tales of on-board life. She had been on one voyage with an ex-Tiller girl who became a little over lubricated and danced on the Captain's Table, not merely one misspent evening, but the unprecipitated entertainment became an unscheduled nightly cabaret turn.

Now she was in her early eighties, we noticed small but insidious changes in her behaviour. She was slower to answer the doorbell. She would be less enthusiastic about taking us around the garden. She was getting a little deaf. She was beginning to repeat herself. Notes were scattered around the house reminding her what she had to do, and then she lost the notes. She had at times sent us an incorrectly addressed envelope. She forgot to send us the usual Christmas box of smoked salmon from Scotland. We would arrive at the house to find that the newspaper she was pretending to read was upside-down on the table.

She would go out in her car out and forget how to get home. I telephoned the Sussex Police to express my concerns, they replied there was nothing they could do until she had an accident.

She was persuaded to be seen by the local doctor. Forewarned and forearmed, she succeeded in putting on a convincing show of apparent sanity and sense. How on earth could he dare to suggest that she were anything but sound of mind, and do have another whisky! He could detect no failing of her mental powers other than slight forgetfulness. He spent perhaps ten minutes with her, and did not, of course, see her wandering about the house at night, replete with more than a little of her favourite tipple, and at great danger to herself.

Used as she was to solitude, when she did have company she tended to relish it and to become an entertaining raconteur. We found that our visits were becoming more relaxed. You still did not really have the opportunity to speak, you listened and laughed – laughed, was this possible? She was my mother, and I had tried so hard to feel some warmth towards her. I admired and respected her for her many achievements in life, but hadn't been able to like her very much. Unbelievably, I was beginning to feel something akin to affection for her.

We'd not at any time had a personal conversation. I had never really known her any more than she had known me. But as she aged and became more frail, she once turned and asked me whether I understood, that 'she had had to do it.' She didn't look for any response. Was she apologising for having left my father, or, perhaps, for the way she had at times spoken to me? I shall never know.

★ ★ ★

My mother's well-being was becoming increasingly dictated by and dependent on her single malts, taken liberally – morning, noon, and night. She would still produce a meal for us, but downgraded from haute cuisine to ham salad with new potatoes, and then ultimately to sandwiches. She poured us coffee but had forgotten to put water in the kettle. She thought the dry coffee quite hilarious and was as amused as we were. She could, mercifully, laugh at herself. We would exchange a perfunctory kiss now on meeting and parting. Was she at last beginning to soften?

Sadly, not. She was still capable of delivering a quick aside, a devastating verbal blow, the sting of the wasp. Her housekeeper had left the ingredients for a simple lunch. I arranged the sandwiches attractively on a serving dish. 'At least you can do *something* right', she barked, to me, a grandmother myself now. At that moment I felt blind fury, not expressed, but no less real. How dare she speak to me like this, how dare she speak to anyone like that, but of course only for me! The verbal attack, the wounding, the enemy of self-esteem.

Perhaps, over all these painful years, if I had been a strong powerful fearless woman like her, confronting her at her own level, verbal gunshot for verbal gunshot, she would have reacted, shown some humanity, been honest with me, let something of herself out. But is that the way of civilised living? I think not. I could not pretend to be something I wasn't. I am happy with myself. Only with her did the mature sensible Cheltenham lady disintegrate backwards into the semblance of a quivering child.

As her health deteriorated, my son Edmund, now married with

children of his own, wanted to visit her once more before she died. Antony and Belle, both under five, sat quietly on a sofa. My mother looked at them but did not speak to them, except through us. She kept asking where they were to be educated. Again and again. As they left, she pointed out to my daughter-in-law Sandra that baby Louis should not have a dummy in "its" mouth, as it would deform "its" jaw. Edmund quietly but very firmly reminded her of the baby's name.

On her ninetieth birthday she was taken out for a beef sandwich and whisky at the local pub, but she was becoming very frail. Everything now was an effort. She no longer took us around her beloved garden. The lemon tree was relegated to the care of her gardener.

On one visit James and I were immediately aware that she knew she had people with her, but had no idea who they were. This was sad and distressing, but the sadness gradually evolved into an overwhelming sensation of relief. The shackles of this difficult relationship I had shared with my mother were instantly severed. We were two women together, and, maybe, we were equals at last.

Now she needed someone to look after her continuously, adamantly refusing to leave her home. Fortunately she had a housekeeper, who went in every day to do everything for her. By now, she could not deal with her affairs, but I knew she had an excellent solicitor.

The end came as I had thought it would. Her solicitor telephoned one Saturday morning. She'd had a fall and was in hospital. I ought to come.

We drove to Sussex at once. She looked dreadful. She was barely conscious. I touched her cheek, but she didn't know me. I questioned the young doctor on duty. He dismissed my anxieties, assuring me that 'it was not as if she was going to die, or anything.'

She died later that night. She was ninety-and-a-half years old.

In the fifty years since she left my father she had not once mentioned his name. I hope perhaps, one day, to discover more about what had motivated this complicated, fearless, and, maybe, troubled woman.

★ ★ ★

Part 13

My father, David, had been born during the First World War, near Stroud. He had never known his grandfather – Alfred. Originating from a family who had worked the land in rural Essex for generations, Alfred had moved to London in the hope of 'bettering himself.' He married a schoolteacher from Bow, studied to be a Professor of Music, and produced four sons. These four sons were therefore the first of the family to enter the professions, one of whom was to become my father's father.

In later researches I discovered that Alfred had played the organ at Whitechapel Church for many years, just down the road from the London Hospital. He and I must have trodden many of the same paths.

The clergy at that time had a position of respect and status in society, but poor monetary reward, and therefore lived in gentile poverty. The class system was rife. What your parents did would almost always dictate your own position in society.

David's mother, with five sisters and a brother, came from a wealthy established Victorian family, all of whom had an excellent education, and most married into similarly professional families. She was besotted with her only son.

He was brought up in the isolated and restricted atmosphere of a country vicarage. There was little travelling, and he was not allowed to play with the other children from the village because they were thought to be unsuitable, and of a lower class to him. His father was a distant uncommunicative figure, and his social circle very restricted and insular.

At the tender age of seven years, financed by his share of the pot of gold, David was sent away to boarding school in the Isle of Wight, not enjoying the experience at all and often sick on the train journey there and back.

During his childhood, his parents kept very much to themselves, with little stimulation from the outside world and with little company for David, other than a plethora of elderly aunts and uncles, or staid people connected with his father's church, thus leading to shyness and insecurity with social situations. He became a quiet sensitive adult, rather solitary, but kind and gentle, like his mother, but because of his discomfiture with people some people found him a little odd.

Although David had not been a high achiever at school, he eventually obtained a good degree in general engineering, leading to a career with a large aircraft-engine manufacturing factory between Cheltenham and Gloucester, where he met my mother, and after a brief courtship, asked her to marry him.

He did his best with the relationship, but having been close to only one woman before – his own gentle mother – he became increasingly overpowered by the dominant nature of his wife. He did not have the courage to assert himself, as any sort of confrontation was utterly alien to him. He would quietly take my side when difficulties arose. He crept around silently, he accepted life as it presented itself every day, desiring only peace and tranquility. He probably never imagined that she would leave him, it not having occurred to him that she might be unhappy, or might have greater expectations from the marriage. Emotions were locked away, each from the other, unknown, unexplored, too dangerous to reveal. He had no motivation to want any more for himself. His reason for living was his work and his daughter, and she became the a central focus of his life.

★ ★ ★

David had been brought up to live frugally, by his parents after the First World War, and by the Government during the Second World War, and for most of his life was reluctant to spend any more than he needed to on any commodity, whether it be a home, a car or a birthday card. Material things were not of importance to him, and he had no aspirations to any preconceived idea of a set standard of living. Where he lived was unimportant, as long as he had a roof over his head, enough to eat, warmth in the winter, a radio and television, and contact with his family. When my mother left him, he decided to move somewhere smaller and nearer to his work. He bought a mobile home in a caravan park, just across the road from his factory.

Clothes lasted for ever. He owned two jackets – a brown Harris tweed for the winter, and an off-white linen for the summer. These two jackets would last, in alternating seasons, for the following sixty years. He kept a suit in the wardrobe, should he ever need to look smart to go somewhere special, but he never did, so there it stayed, with his trilby hat, which he never wore. And an umbrella which he never put up. And a suitcase for going away, which he never did.

In winter, he would heat and live in one room only, while the icicles would form exotic patterns on the windows of the adjoining room. When his shoes fell apart he would fix them with superglue. When his belt broke he used string. He sent me unsigned birthday and Christmas cards so that I could send them on to someone else, or back to him. He shared a birthday with the Queen Mother, so always, tongue-in-cheek, assumed that the BBC was playing the National Anthem especially for him. He was quietly proud of his initiative in his methods of cost-cutting, and found the whole subject amusing. It wasn't as if he were poverty stricken, it was good husbandry and doing your bit for the country. He lived in his cold drab little residence for many years, until he retired from his work, but he seemed content, and demanded nothing more from anyone. You couldn't change him, or how he chose to live. That was the way he was.

David had a deep-rooted sense of responsibility and loyalty towards his mother, his daughter, and his grandchildren when they were born, but still his everyday existence was a solitary one. In spite of this, he did occasionally make a friend – invariably a woman. He never actively sought the companionship of men, but was comfortable enough with them if their company was thrust upon him.

When he did allow someone into his strange but open-hearted world, that person would remain loyal for years and would always remain in touch, and have sincere fondness for him. One neighbouring lady used to give him raspberries every year from her garden. She became the 'raspberry woman' and I heard about her for years.

He had a wonderful sense of silly humour, almost childish, and this endeared him to people. Because he loved cats, he had an assortment of cuddly toy felines, mostly given as gifts. Every Christmas they would have gold crowns placed on their heads, in celebration. Three of them instantly became the Maji, ready to bear gifts to the remaining felines. Bosscat was the chief cat. Bosscat was allowed to fraternise with his girlfriend cat occasionally, but not too often, and only discreetly. Sometimes they really misbehaved at night, I was told.

My father had always run a car, but as the years went by the standard of vehicle diminished. They would be borderline roadworthy. Would it pass the Ministry of Transport test or not? Usually not, and his local garage would do intricate things with Plastic Padding to prevent his feet going through the floor. Owning and driving a vehicle was not only of great use in transporting him on visits to the family, but was also an interest, something to discuss and provided entertainment and a challenge every year.

He was a very cautious driver. His normal speed would be 35 m.p.h. On a day when he was feeling particularly daring, and with a strong tail wind, this might reach forty. There must have been many a frustrated driver behind him on the A36 for many years. Although he was so little travelled (he had never even been to London until latterly) and unused to company, he would courageously take the train from Cheltenham to regularly visit us in Kent, involving both underground and mainline changes in London, which he soon mastered, and would stay with us for a few days.

My father loved his grandchildren and would follow their progress avidly, never failing to show interest and encouragement and his pride in their achievements. He would join in any activities, from country walks to chess and board games. Always kind, always gentle, always anxious not to upset feelings, he would know when to remain quiet and keep his own counsel. He would not speak about himself very much as other people were more important to him. Having lived on his own for so long, conversation in itself was a great pleasure for him.

David had always visited his parents frequently. When his father died from peritonitis, having failed to tell anyone he had a pain until it was too late, he became even more devoted to his mother, and would take her out in the car every week, it didn't matter where, just to give her a diversion from the loneliness of her home. His family were of the 'old school', so was proud and unwilling to ask for help. He was on his own.

As his mother's health gradually deteriorated he looked after her himself for as long as he could. She was to suffer three successive strokes, resulting in protracted and stressful periods in nursing homes, all of which David bore with fortitude, and much sadness. She didn't know who he was for the last two years or so.

I went to visit my grandmother. She didn't know me either. He didn't tell me of her death till some time after. At her funeral only David and the vicar were present. How sad, how alone.

★ ★ ★

Life went on, and my father continued to see his remaining family, which now became the main purpose and interest of his life. He retired at the age of sixty-five, having assembled aircraft engine component parts for forty-five years for both Rolls-Royce and de Havilland, a massive number of parts for a massive number of engines. On his death certificate the registrar advised me to enter his occupation as an 'aircraft propulsion engineer', which would have amused him enormously.

He had the regulatory watch, golden handshake, and a reasonable pension, which he had no intention of spending on himself. So he stayed in his mobile home, living his solitary life, generally unmotivated to any great activity, but quite content in the idleness of his retirement and his periodic visits from 'lady friends'. He wrote copious letters to them and to us, every one typed laboriously on his well worn and battered typewriter, which was still serving him well when the rest of us had progressed to personal computers. We had to travel miles to find replacement ribbons, and the young men from whom we bought them would observe these items with wonder, incredulous that anyone should still be using such objects of antiquity.

He was a very talented and mentally astute chess player, and would spend hours playing himself – sometimes he won, sometimes he lost.

In his seventies my father was still living in his mobile home, and still driving, but arthritis was setting in, and life was getting harder. He was less mobile, but he still enjoyed his visits to us, and would sometimes have our cats for us when we were on holiday, which made him feel useful, which, indeed, he was.

One day while driving out to do his shopping he had a slight altercation with a district nurse and her car. He turned right into the main road – he should have waited; she was approaching from the left. He was moving so slowly that she could not help but hit the back of his car. Though he thoroughly enjoyed meeting the pleasant young nurse, the slight accident shook his confidence, and he wisely decided to give up driving when he reached the age of eighty.

★ ★ ★

Part 14

My mother, Grace, was born into a working-class family, but from an early age she had shown a certain innate ambition and strength of character, an individuality, a fire in her belly. She was different to the other girls in her village. In truth, her achievements in life were to prove that she was a woman born, in many respects, before her time.

She had an elementary education at the village school, with no opportunity of any further education. This lack of education was going to be a catalyst for one of the motivating forces in her future life.

She left home as soon as she could, to earn money and to follow her ambition of 'making something of herself,' and by the time she met my father she had already worked her way up to a managerial role, quickly promoted to the position of Staff Catering Manageress at the aircraft engine production company near Cheltenham.

David was a very good-looking man and there was an immediate mutual attraction. As the relationship developed, she was to learn of his background, totally different to hers. She agreed to marry him, aware that, by doing so, she was giving herself an introduction into a much higher level of society, a different class of family.

The marriage became both constricting and frustrating for such a free spirited, quick thinking, independent woman, but, doing the right thing as always, she gave of her best, in the only way she knew. While she would soon recognise the personal mismatch between herself and my father, she also realised that the marriage could give her the opportunity to follow her quest of self education, if only so that she could meet her assumed extended family on apparently equal terms. Her clerical father-in-law, especially, university-educated and highly intellectual, provided an immediate challenge, and she needed to be able to converse with the rest of his family, who were all well educated and au fait with the world.

She became increasingly aware of the great social and cultural divide between the refined gentility of David's family and the poor uneducated unworldliness of her own. The two families had not met.

She started to read. She cultivated the 'right people', not only for her daughter's sake, but for her own, to listen, to learn, to seek to reach the pinnacle of social acceptability. She took a deeper interest in the theatre, and gradually became more adept in conversing on a similar intellectual plane to that of her newly acquired family, even though there were huge vacuums in her knowledge of the arts.

An understanding and appreciation of music, literature, and art, fared poorly in Suffolk Square, but in the homes of the aunts and uncles there would invariably be a piano, usually never played, a symbol of status and culture which gathered dust under a profusion of sepia family photographs in silver frames. There would also be a library-full of dusty volumes of literature ancient and modern, not often read but known about, and a few watercolours or oils from the gifted hands of reputable artists. Impeccable good taste.

They named their child 'Heather', after a child from David's home village whom they thought a 'nice little girl', and 'Joan' after his mother, and were very happy with her arrival.

Grace was not a natural mother, and would never be able to forget herself enough to enter a child's world. Any child was labelled "it" until he or she was able to conduct a reasonably intelligent conversation with her. She was too impatient, she did not have the time or patience to wait, to listen, to pay attention. Her own train of thought and activity was too energetic and unstoppable. It was well looked after, often being left in its perambulator in the garden in the front of Number Five Suffolk Square, by the magnolia tree, for passers-by to stop and admire. When it was three, she bundled it into a chair on the back of a bicycle, and took it to kindergarten for the mornings, releasing time for herself.

She would rarely be idle. At home all day, she would always keep busy and occupied. One of her most gifted skills was as a needle-woman, and she made not only clothes for herself and her daughter, but also exquisitely smocked dresses for little girls. Every bodice of each little dress, made from a fabric called 'dayella', would be smocked by hand, painstakingly and perfectly finished. A revolutionary idea for the time, Grace turned this venture into a successful mail-order business. This was a start to earning her living and creating some independence for herself.

She also possessed an inborn social conscience, and while striving to improve and educate herself she was never to forget those born without the privileges of money and education. She was a very domestically-skilled and practical woman, and would assist her neighbours if needed. If illness struck, she would be there with homemade soup and advice. She could turn her hand to anything, she was a 'coper.'

It was soon apparent to her that there was going to be little warmth or companionship in her marriage, but you did your duty, kept busy, and got on with life. She was polite to David, but there was little or no mutual respect or affection.

Heather was now at preparatory school and she could begin to think of going out to work. David generally worked nights, and could be there for her during the day. She still took her daughter down to the main bus station every morning for her journey to Seven Springs and would pick her up at the end of the day.

Having made a point of being a churchgoer, for reasons rather alien to those of being a committed Christian, she involved herself with some of its activities. She ran a group which was run by the local church, called the 'Girls' Friendly Society', whose ethos was that young girls from all backgrounds were taught Christian morals and standards, and encouraged to participate in various activities. Being a born organiser, she proved to be excellent at this. She would enter her girls in County drama festivals, producing plays and poetry readings. She taught them baking, first aid, useful things. The learning of these skills gave them confidence and broadened their outlook, and thus encouraged them to face their futures with optimism borne of self-belief.

She made friends in the Square, if a little selectively, and kept busy. She had stamina and courage, and "you just got on with things."

★ ★ ★

When Heather started at the College, Grace was presented with a new level of freedom. David was at work or in bed, the marriage was suppressing her mentally and emotionally, and she had to find her own motivation and fulfilment in life.

She had also worked for several years, in a voluntary capacity, for the local Civil Defence Corps, so had built up considerable experience in all aspects of its work. She studied and attended courses, striving to make amends for her lack of formal education.

She applied for the position of Chief Civil Defence Officer for the county of Gloucester, and was offered the job, the first woman in the country to have achieved this position of seniority in that organisation. She was now, by virtue of her work and the professional people she was meeting, equalling the status of David's family, and she had every reason to be proud of her remarkable achievement.

Grace worked like a Trojan, and was totally committed to her new career. She had left David behind in every way. Every challenge motivated her further and more strongly, and her energy was limitless. At last she had an opportunity to use her excellent brain to its full potential, and put into action her outstanding qualities as a leader, and decision-maker. She was forceful and persuasive and stood no nonsense from anybody. Her work schedule included running courses for the public, training them to deal with emergency situations of any kind. This included the giving of lectures on the potentially horrifying and graphic effects of nuclear fallout and what action to take, and the reasons why.

The devastating floods at Tewkesbury and the surrounding areas of Gloucestershire in the early fifties presented an enormous and perilous civilian challenge. A state of emergency was proclaimed. Combined with the other emergency services, she commandeered her crew and set forth to the devastated region, with no thought to her own safety. She was at her best in command of others. She and her team assisted in rescuing those trapped in their homes, and in the organisation of rest centres where the evacuees could be fed and housed until the danger had passed, and the waters had receded.

It was during this time that she met John and this was to alter the course of her life. He was based in Warwick, doing the equivalent of her job in that county. The attraction was immediate. They both attended a civil defence conference in Paris. They had fallen in love, and knew that, whatever the consequences, they had to be together.

However, although my mother was trapped in a meaningless marriage, her sense of duty prevailed. She was not going to consider leaving David until Heather left home. She could then do so with a clear conscience.

★ ★ ★

Part 15

*M*y mother and John moved to a sleepy hamlet in Warwickshire, and embarked on a relationship which was to be a source of great happiness to them both, and which would endure for thirty years until John died. She stepped into the elevated role of country squire's wife with ease, reaping the benefits of her earlier years spent studying the manners and mores of the upper-classes. Her working years as a senior officer, meeting a wide cross-section of people from all backgrounds, and with a fair degree of travel had widened her horizons and given her a comprehensive awareness of the world. She had overcome the class divide with flying colours.

Although they did not socialise to any great extent, they would happily pass the time of day with people who lived in the village. They did, indeed, live in material comfort and a considerable degree of affluence, but the life they led was not one of profligacy or ostentation. They had both experienced the plight of the underprivileged in the course of their work, and were aware, my mother especially, what it was like to struggle in life, to know real hardship and harsh beginnings, not to have opportunities, and to have limited hope of success in life. They had come across talented youngsters, especially in the poorer rural parts of the counties, who did not have access to the finance necessary to fund further studies or training.

They were generous. A young boy turned up at the front gates one day, a 'Bob a Job' volunteer looking for a job. John set him to work painting some railings, and they were both so impressed with the excellence of the boy's work that they asked him to come back and do more work, and got to know his family. They ended up years later quietly funding him to go to Harvard to study law.

She stayed in touch with her daughter and her family and would write at Christmas and birthdays, and try to welcome them if they came to see her. She did not encourage the visits – it embarrassed and troubled her to be reminded of her first marriage. She could not dispel her guilt at having left David in the way she did, and the effect it must have had on her daughter.

★ ★ ★

John became ill. He had cancer and was not given long to live. My mother nursed him devotedly at home. He had a massive haemorrhage. She stood over the doctor, who was ready with a shot of morphine. Maybe he gave John just a little bit more than he should have done. Nobody argued with my mother.

Ten days later the nineteen-eighties hurricane struck, hitting Sussex particularly badly. A large tree was uprooted and came down on my mother's roof. Many trees on the estate were down, and the damage extensive. It was a terrible time for her. Local people rallied round to help her, but coming to terms with loneliness was difficult.

She was proud but vulnerable, and could not stay in the enormous house with its extensive grounds and maintenance. It was far too much to manage alone, and the risks of intrusion and burglary were too great. She was advised to move and heeded the advice.

My mother was a strong woman, and you carried on. She made gallant efforts to socialise and to meet her few neighbours. They were mainly widows, of similar wealth and status to herself, and lonely, but far too proud to admit it. There was one younger family, and the wife, in her early forties, took on the role of 'domestic help' for her, eventually being promoted to full-time housekeeper, and becoming a valued helper and friend. She also employed a gardener two or three days a week, so she had contact with people, albeit that nothing or nobody could fill the cavernous gap left by John's death.

She wanted to create some lasting memorial to him – something that would reflect her aspirations towards creating a better world for the disadvantaged in society, which she knew he had cared about as much as she did.

With expert legal and professional advice, she went about setting up an educational trust, founded in his name. Its purpose was to fund bursaries and grants for any young person who, because of the circumstances of his or her background, would not otherwise have the opportunity to benefit from further education. It would encompass not only those with academic promise, but also gifted young musicians, performers, or artists.

This became a raison d'être, as she took an active role in the inauguration of the registered charity, and the appointment of a governing board of professionals to oversee it. She would take a keen interest in its work, as one of the board members, attending six-monthly meetings which involved the assessment of finances with bankers, and selection of potential beneficiaries.

Following the shock of John's death, she had gradually reverted to presenting herself to others as the grande dame, with manner both intimidating and domineering. This could alienate people newly-acquainted to her. She had no time for people whose intellects she considered to be inferior to her own. Unsurprisingly, she did not make friends easily.

She was persuaded to attend the local Women's Institute meetings, doing the right thing, but had not the patience to listen to talks on subjects on which she herself could have lectured infinitely better. Her mind was quick, her temper short. She went to church for a time, but profoundly disagreed with the exhortations from the pulpit of this particular vicar, and eventually stopped attending services, but not before she had told him something of her life and her background.

She still went to the theatre occasionally, taking the train from Lewes to Victoria. She went on her cruises, encouraged by similarly-placed widowed acquaintances, who, I suspect, were very keen to spend her money. She lived life as fully as she could without John, and still attended the meetings of the Trust, but it was all becoming more of an effort.

Heather and James came to see her, but it became harder and harder to find the energy to cope with the visits. She did her best to entertain them well, to welcome them, to show interest, and to do everything correctly.

She slowed down, no longer walking in the forest every day, or tending to her garden, or caring too much about her lemon tree, or going out much. She stopped driving. She had a couple of bouts of severe bronchitis, and was short of breath sometimes.

As she reached her late eighties, she did less and less. She stayed at home. Her beloved labrador 'Meg' had to be put to sleep. She did not replace her. She was repeating herself. She could not remember where things were, and what people were called.

On her ninetieth birthday she was taken out for a beef sandwich and her favourite tipple, but she was telling people that she was 'ready to go.'

She was in the kitchen. She had her usual tipple, and a little supper. She could not remember falling.

Everything was very black now.

★ ★ ★

My emotions and thoughts had been in turmoil for my mother's last year or two before her death, but in the final analysis the explanation for our fraught relationship was perhaps, in many ways, explicable. She had, of course, been disappointed in my failure to reach the pinnacle of a learned profession, which would have atoned to a degree for her missed opportunities due to her lack of education, but that alone was not enough to cause the fragile and shallow nature of our relationship. Her intelligence was astute, but her inner self could not handle closeness with another human being, especially her daughter, to whom she could, and should, have been closest.

She had proved for herself that anything in life is possible, whatever your level of education, if you are ambitious and determined to work hard, so there was no reason for regret or unhappiness in her own achievements.

What had caused her guarded and unapproachable manner? Was it, indeed, the fear of the exposure of hidden truths? There must have been no small measure of guilt – in the manner in which she had abandoned her marriage, and her husband, who, in her opinion, was a weak and unambitious man, but to me was a devoted and loving father. Surely, too, the lifelong rift with her own birth family must have caused her deep anguish at times. Had she considered herself too good for them? Social status then being of such significance, and so potentially divisive, did she take it upon herself to decide that her family was likely to be an embarrassment to her when she married into an upper-class family? Did she consider them to be beneath her? If that was the case, the superficial shallowness and callousness of her reasoning at the time must, surely, as the long years progressed, have shamed her.

Why did she not let me know immediately that John had died? Was she afraid of letting me see her human frailty, the real and deep-felt depth of her grief? Was she angry, aware that the only person with whom she had a fulfilling relationship had gone?

Did she feel sadness at the long periods of impasse with her daughter, did she regret the lack of contact with her two grandsons, now both successful and charmingly personable adults, who could have done so much for her, had she wanted it?

The price was high. Her family would have liked to have known her, but she would not let any of us near her real self.

The questions refuse to disappear, but now is the time to come to terms with the past, to remember the good times, to forgive, and to accept that, in all aspects of her life, my mother did what she thought was right.

★ ★ ★

Part 16

James and I had seen a bungalow for sale at the other end of our village. We suggested to David that he might move here to be nearer us, now that he was dispensing with his car. Knowing him to be so fiercely independent, we were surprised and pleased when he agreed.

I like to think that this final phase was the happiest and most comfortable of his life. We had a small party to celebrate his eightieth birthday. His grandsons travelled from both ends of the country to be with him, it was a happy day. He would see us whenever he wanted, and we were there if he needed help.

He loved his new home. You could press a button and have instant heat. It was the first time in his life that he had been properly warm. He descended into a hermetically-sealed existence from that moment of discovery, and lived every hour of his remaining days at a constant seventy-five degrees Fahrenheit, or over.

He saw more people than ever before. He was still intrinsically solitary and private, but was beginning to realise the pleasures of companionship and regular human contact. Neighbours would visit, bringing him pancakes, hot cross buns, and Christmas cake on the appropriate days. They were kind to a man whom they perceived as being a little reserved, but always behaving as befits a 'gentleman.' He was very appreciative, and became quite friendly with one or two of them. They warmed to his sense of the ridiculous and his silly sense of fun, and his genuine interest in themselves and their lives.

David also succeeded in curbing his lack of spending which had prevailed over the previous half-century. He would now freely purchase any item which he needed, without a detailed cost analysis. His attention to birthdays became legendary, and he would spend days, if not weeks, in the planning of the correct card and present for the recipient. He had never been mean, but now the price of the gift would no longer be the overriding issue. But he would still sometimes give unsigned Christmas cards, to be recycled the following year.

He always kept well informed about world affairs. He would pretend he was becoming a little 'dotty' to amuse people and become endearingly silly, but the following day would discuss the minutiae of politics and the state of current share markets. His mind was always sharp, and he would enjoy sensible discussion as much as the trivial.

Long hours would be spent together playing chess or draughts. He was an excellent player and would be many strategic moves ahead of me. If crashing defeat was imminent, he would immediately announce a draw. He could not bear to see me lose.

He and James got on very well. They shared a happy and optimistic disposition. It was probably the closest relationship David had with a man. They were both very practical. David had once made a dolls' house out of two tea chests – the result was a magnificent residence, complete with a working plumbing system – running water from the taps and a lavatory which flushed. James, too, was extremely skilled with his hands and carved rocking horses which were greatly admired. He made David an inlaid chess table with which he was delighted, and various gadgets to help him when mobility became difficult. One was a personally inscribed long wooden leg scratcher for when David was in bed and could not reach his itching legs – trivial but invaluable.

These happy years were drawing to their close. He was not wanting to leave his bungalow anymore – the effort involved was too much, and he progressed from using a walking aid to a wheelchair – increasingly in pain and discomfort but never complaining.

One day in his late eighties my father took to his bed, never to leave it again. He did not feel ill, simply very tired, and that was the only place where he could be comfortable. For these final two years, he still had his television and radio, so kept in contact with the world. Staff from a care agency came in to help look after him. He found this intrusive at first, but soon came to welcome their visits. He wanted to stay at home, if possible, whatever the future held for him.

As he gradually became increasingly frail, we would talk, and talk, and talk. His mind would go back in time – his childhood, his mother, his father whom he didn't really know, anything and everything.

He hardly mentioned my mother in all these years. He did reiterate that their attraction had been essentially physical and that they had married, unwisely, in haste. And he thought 'she had not been a very good mother.' The subject was too emotive and he was not really comfortable talking about it. He expressed his regret when she died. I thought that he was being very gracious and forgiving in his words. Because my mother was as she was, he had endured a miserable marriage as much as I had endured an anxiety-ridden childhood.

I understood him well, and feel that as he was such an intrinsically kind and sensitive man, he would never have voiced his innermost thoughts, or expressed bitterness or hurt – to such a private man there were things you just don't talk about. I think that his feelings towards my mother, soon after the initial thrill and lust of a wartime affair, dwindled into apathy and tired resignation.

It was a relief to me that my father's past experiences of life with my mother so many years before had never appeared to embitter him, towards her personally, or to women in general. In fact he genuinely liked, and laughed with, and respected women – the seed probably having been sown by his very great love and closeness to his mother.

I had never really known the man he was at the time, because of his introversion in a stifled relationship, with the subsequent cramping of his true character. Over the years I had him to myself and my family, I grew to appreciate what a funny and sensitive person he was, and how he had come to terms with his solitary life in such a gracious and dignified manner. And how his concern was always for other people, not himself.

I had always wanted to ask him whether they were forced into marriage due to a child being on the way, but considered it far too intrusive and embarrassing a question. It was surprisingly comforting to eventually discover, from the marriage certificate in my mother's papers, that I was born ten months after the marriage.

★ ★ ★

I knew the end was near when David didn't take much notice of my birthday – he'd always made a fuss over the occasion. And then we had been away for the weekend, normally he would have asked endless questions about what we had done, where we had been, but no longer.

He was getting weaker. He was put on the doctor's priority list of 'unlikely to live for more than six weeks,' guaranteeing extra nursing and the provision of anything he needed.

He was philosophical. He did not believe in an afterlife. He was glad I was with James.

His favourite photographs of the family were placed strategically on the wall in front of his bed – the first thing to see in the morning and the last at night.

During his last evening he thanked me for being there. I wanted to thank him for being a constant and affectionate friend for sixty-six years, but words failed me when I needed them most.

He died the following afternoon. He, too, was ninety-and-a-half years old.

★ ★ ★

When we arrived for my mother's funeral, her solicitor, Adam, called me to one side before the service and warned me that I might have a few surprises. He had already unearthed a few private documents.

The church about half-full, which was quite a respectable turnout. We sat down. The vicar entered his pulpit to give the eulogy.

What was this? Was I in the wrong church? This was surely not my mother's life he was describing?

It appeared that she was the daughter of a vicar, the father of a large family, all of whom had been privately-educated. She had then, apparently, become a teacher and had spent many years following her profession both in this country and abroad. She had then, when still quite young, met and married John and they had inherited their estate to become wealthy landowners.

No mention of her first marriage, or daughter, or grandsons. No mention of her excellent career in civil defence. Extraordinary.

Her solicitor and myself were the only two people in the congregation who were witness to the untruths spoken.

I silently asked God to forgive her for her lies, but to remember her for her deeply-felt humanitarian instinct – exemplified by all the good she had done for other people during her lifetime, and would, by her legacy, so continue to do.

At the after-service assembly at the old brickyard, with flag drooping sadly at half-mast, most of the mourners seemed surprised to discover there was a daughter – sometimes I wondered myself, whether I was a figment of my mother's imagination.

★ ★ ★

I tried to analyse my feelings after her death. Jane had written a letter of sympathy to me, explaining that she would remember my mother for her 'affection, compassion, wisdom, and encouragement.' She did, indeed, possess these human virtues in great measure, but as a woman, not as a mother.

Of course I was very grateful for all the practical care she had given me as I grew up, and the fact that she had stayed with my father for so long in order not to destroy the family unit, dysfunctional though it was, until I was an adult. But what you remember are the emotional issues, the turmoil of feelings, the complexities of misunderstandings unaddressed and unresolved.

I felt sadness that we had never been able to become friends, to relax in one anothers company, to share a joke.

I felt admiration for the fearless way she had met life 'head on', determined to do the best with the circumstances of the day, and the way she had managed to convince everyone she met, albeit with some dishonesty, that she was a lady born and bred.

I felt anger, which still lingers like a low-grade infection which will not go away, for the manner in which she treated me – the constant criticism and lack of encouragement, and destruction of self-esteem, which I considered unjustifiable and undeserved.

I felt bewilderment that we, two sensible women, could not realise that something was so wrong, and could not seem to care enough to want to make it better.

I felt frustration that she had no idea of the hurt that she had caused through the years.

I felt relief, though I am ashamed to admit it, that the mental anguish of trying to maintain such a disappointing relationship for six long decades was finally over, and I could move forward, in the knowledge that I had done my best.

Nurture a plant and it will flourish, but apply too much of an inappropriate pesticide and it will be damaged.

★ ★ ★

Part 17

James and I returned to Cheltenham, fifty years later, a kind of final pilgrimage. Neptune's fountain was dry and the planting in the parks and gardens did not seem as vivid and profuse as I had remembered. 'Remember it's only March,' said the charming lady in the Tourist Office.

Cavendish House still graces the Promenade, surrounded by top quality shops and designer outlets, and now there is an impressive Regency arcade, again with a plethora of shops and restaurants. There is a cosmopolitan feel, the image of the town is different. It is alive, it is chic, there is an atmosphere of multicultural sophistication. Coffee from every corner of the globe, award-winning restaurants, cafés, surely reminiscent of Paris or Brussels.

And how fares Suffolk Square? It looks a trifle neglected and unloved now. Where the colonels who used to live there would clip their hedges and tend their gardens with military precision, the present incumbents mainly rent the flats, and do not have the same degree of time. They are busy with their studies at the nearby schools and colleges.

But they have fixed the verandah roof of Number Five, and the magnolia outside is prolific and in bloom. The bowling green endures as the focal point of the square, and our old house next to the church has changed to offices. The church – can this be possible? – is now an Italian restaurant of gastronomic renown.

Suffolk Parade is transformed – buzzing now with antique shops, art galleries, bistros with tables spilling onto the street – how bohemian.

How continental it feels – I could be back in Montmartre in the artists' quarter. And the dear old Daffodil is still there, but transformed into an arts centre and a sophisticated restaurant. How good that the name was retained.

The fountain is probably in full flow again now. The horse lovers and socialites will flock to the races, the literary and artistic intelligentsia will enjoy their festivals, the theatre goers will love their theatre, and the aspiring minds of the future will be finely educated.

The Ladies' College retains its excellence, deeply-rooted on the site where the spa waters were first discovered, the sheer magnificence of its Gothic Hall and domes and turrets and towers unappreciated by the schoolgirl of fifty years ago.

Of the procession of green girls who pass through its portals, some will soar with outstanding success to become politicians, writers, artists, musicians, doctors, scientists, lawyers, the leaders of others. Others will follow lesser professional paths and destinies, but all will be well-grounded in social responsibility, the importance of being true to yourself, and of making the best of the talents and opportunities you have, with the hope of making some impression on the world, however minor.

And, for generations to come, the majestic horse chestnuts will drop their conkers around the shoppers in the Promenade.

All is well in Cheltenham.

★ ★ ★

Part 18

Postscript

My mother was born in a terraced workers' cottage, long since demolished, in a remote Gloucestershire village. It was wartime. Times were hard, supplies were short, and poverty prevailed. Most of the men were away fighting, and every day life was tough for the women left to look after their homes and families. Conditions at home were primitive.

Her parents, Arthur and Clara, named their daughter 'Grace'. She went to the local village elementary school, leaving as early as possible to get work and earn money, with no question of any further education.

Soon after her marriage to David she ceased all contact with her family, thereby disowning her roots completely. She would see none of them again.

On meeting John, she created for herself a new identity, with which to face her new role in the 'upper classes.' She changed her name, by deed poll, adopting John's surname and choosing a new Christian name – Diana. She invented a fictitious life story, informing people that she was a vicar's daughter who had been a teacher, and that she had travelled extensively abroad before her marriage.

After her death, Adam and I delved into her papers. The truth was revealed. Her father had been the village carpenter, descended from a long line of builders, plumbers, and glaziers, who had originated from Somerset. Further research revealed that her immediate family, at the time of the estrangement, consisted of her parents, her grandparents, two uncles, one aunt, an older brother, William, and a younger – another Arthur. All the men of the family were, or had been, in the building and affiliated trades, but her aunt, ironically, had been a schoolteacher.

Adam found it incredible to discover that the gentrified couple whom he and his parents had known for years at the 'Big House' were not at the time legally married, and therefore were barely-respectable in the eyes of traditional middle-Englanders of assumedly unblemished morals. As my mother's solicitor, he had spent lengthy periods of time with her over the years, and he was as amazed as I was to uncover the barrelfull of lies she had fabricated about her past life, as well as to discover that when my mother and John eventually married, just before his death, she had reached the age of seventy-two. We sat together over a reviving drink, crumpled and revealing documents before us, and thought it would make a good story, and had another drink. We felt that she had had the last laugh over us all. She had taken her final curtain and had left the stage.

He was shocked that so many of the things he had known about my mother had proved to be false, and I was shocked and sad that, even in the days when social class could be such a divisive issue, she had felt the need to abandon her roots and invent such a fictitious story.

Adam was the soul of discretion, and never uttered a word to anyone, not even to his parents, and nor did I, except to my immediate family.

Both Diana's grandmother and aunt were named 'Elizabeth'. This is my middle name. It is the only connection I have with a family I was never given the opportunity to know.

I succeeded in tracing her only surviving younger brother, Arthur, who still lives in Gloucestershire. He had not heard from his sister, 'Grace' to him, since he left the army at the end of the war, soon after her marriage. I told him of her death. He was surprised and shocked to hear of her after so long, but glad to hear something of her life. We are still in contact. Maybe he alone could have added a piece or two to the jigsaw, if he had been prepared to discuss what she was like as a child and the circumstances of her departure from the family, but that did not happen. I felt that it was impossible to intrude to that degree by cross-questioning a very old man, so I told him what I thought he wanted to hear – that she had been a good mother and that I would miss her. There is so much I cannot and will not tell him.

Did John know of her true background? Probably not. Nobody else did. Even Jane, who had known her for over fifty years, had been told lies about her early years. When Jane discovered this I know she felt betrayed, that the long-lasting friendship which she had valued had been devoid of total honesty.

★ ★ ★

The Educational Trust is healthily solvent, and will enable many deserving young people to fulfil their educational or artistic potential for generations to come.

And, vulgar though it is for a lady to talk of money, you might ask – did Diana leave any of her massive pot of inherited gold to me, the answer is – a little, as always doing the right thing, but the bulk of it went, quite appropriately, to the trust she had founded, and to several other worthy charitable causes of her choice.

However, she left me her jewellery case.

Among the gems was a sizeable diamond, exquisitely cut, set in a silver brooch.

I sold it. The final bidder was a private jeweller – from Cheltenham.

★ ★ ★

Lightning Source UK Ltd.
Milton Keynes UK
22 September 2009

144010UK00001B/41/P